VOICES FROM THE SEA

"My real log is written in the sea and the sky.... It has gradually come to life out of all that has surrounded us for months: the sounds of water on the hull, the sounds of wind gliding on the sails, the silences full of secret things between my boat and me."

— Bernard Moitessier

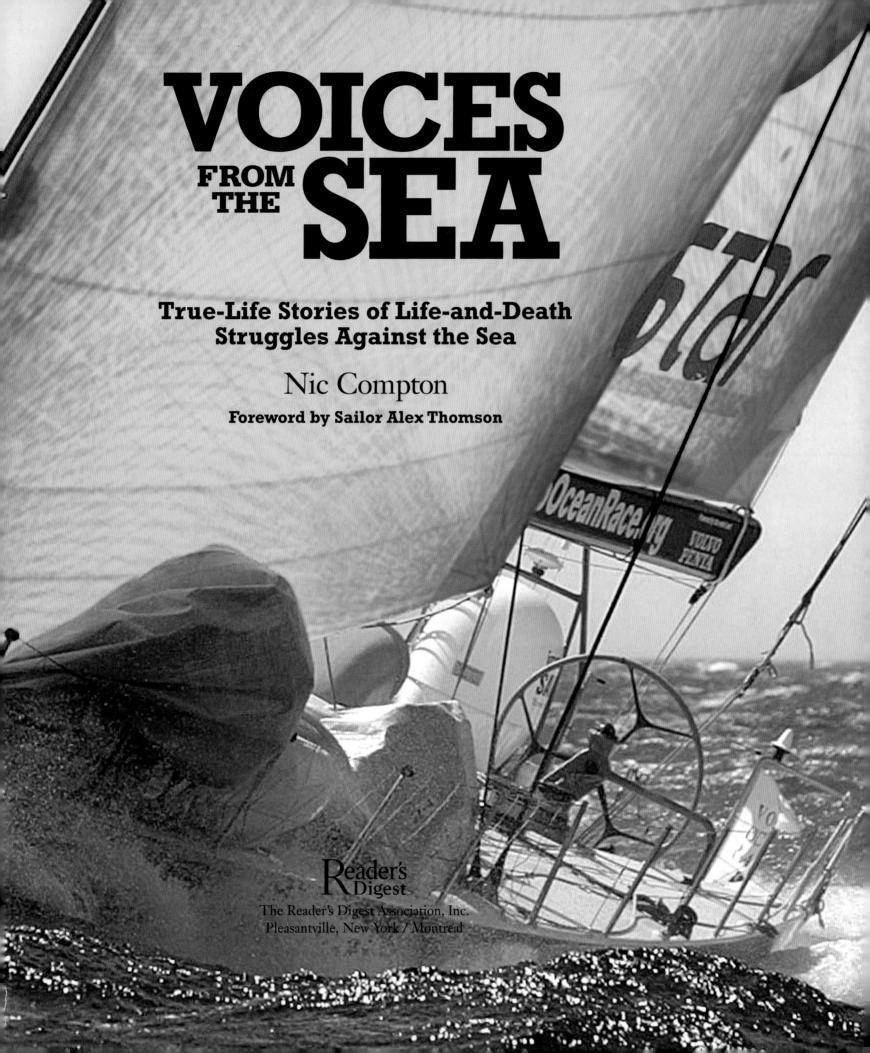

VOICES
FROM THE SEA

True-Life Stories of Life-and-Death Struggles Against the Sea

Nic Compton

Foreword by Sailor Alex Thomson

Reader's Digest

The Reader's Digest Association, Inc.
Pleasantville, New York / Montreal

A READER'S DIGEST BOOK

This edition published by The Reader's Digest Association, Inc., by arrangement with Cassell Illustrated, Octopus Publishing Group, London 2008
A Hachette Livre UK company

FOR CASSELL ILLUSTRATED

Project Editor: Fiona Kellagher
Commissioning Editor: Laura Price
Designer: Tony Cohen
Picture Researcher: Jennifer Veall

FOR READER'S DIGEST

U.S. Project Editors: Barbara Booth, Kim Casey
Canadian Project Editors: Jim Hynes, Pamela Johnson
Project Designer: Jennifer Tokarski
Associate Art Director: George McKeon
Executive Editor, Trade Publishing: Dolores York
Associate Publisher: Roseanne McManus
President and Publisher, Trade Publishing: Harold Clarke

Library of Congress Cataloging-in-Publication Data:

Compton, Nic.
Voices from the sea : True-life stories of life-and-death struggles against the sea / Nic Compton.
     p. cm.
"A Reader's Digest book."
ISBN-10: 0-7621-0865-7
ISBN-13: 978-0-7621-0865-7
1.   Seafaring life--Anecdotes.   I. Title.
G540.C6665 2007
910.4'5--dc22
2007019999

We are committed to both the quality of our products and the service we provide to our customers. We value your comments, so please feel free to contact us:

The Reader's Digest Association, Inc.
Adult Trade Publishing
Reader's Digest Road
Pleasantville, NY 10570-7000

For more Reader's Digest products and information, visit our website:
www.rd.com (in the United States)
www.readersdigest.ca (in Canada)

Printed in China

1 3 5 7 9 10 8 6 4 2

Contents

# **Foreword**

I was delighted to be asked to write the foreword for a book containing such outstanding stories. Some of these tales are legendary; others are quite new to me but all of them describe the uniqueness of our oceans and how frail human life is within them.

I have an unconscious desire to spend as much time as possible at sea. At an early age I started windsurfing and dinghy sailing, and I learned to wake board and water ski. More recently I have mastered kite surfing, and they are all just my hobbies. My day job is aboard one of the most powerful racing machines afloat, an Open 60, often racing around the world single- or double-handed. I consider this to be my job, very much the way a doctor, plumber, or a factory worker would. There are parts of the job I love, parts that are OK, and frankly, parts that I loathe.

The Southern Ocean is a love/hate place for me. It provides the most fantastic, exhilarating sailing on the planet, but it is also one of the most inhospitable places in our world. Relentless winds build up unremitting waves with freezing temperatures and hazards such as icebergs ready to cut through your steed like a knife through butter. As time goes by, the days feel relatively safe but the nights are like an extended game of Russian roulette! I have been to the Southern Ocean three times and have suffered a hole in my boat, two dismastings, and in the Velux 5 Oceans, I abandoned my boat, took to my life raft, and was rescued by Mike Golding; yet I will go back again, both single- and double-handed. Why, you may ask?

The following pages describe unfathomable tales of attempting and often achieving what most ordinary people would consider impossible or even ridiculous. Why would someone want to windsurf across the Indian Ocean, kite surf across the Atlantic, or put themselves in a position where they have to sew up a gash in his or her own tongue? Human beings have always strived to achieve, to be the first, to break the record, and our oceans provide the most difficult environments in which to do this. The cold, heat, fierce waves, flat calms, and most of all, the unpredictability, provide a dangerous playground in which to achieve the unachievable, beat the unbeatable, and ultimately test ourselves to the limit and beyond.

The first man landed on the moon in 1969. A few months later Sir Robin Knox-Johnston became the first person to sail nonstop around the world single-handed. Over 1,800 people have climbed to the top of the world, Mt. Everest, yet just sixty men and women have sailed single-handed nonstop around our planet. This surely puts their bravery into perspective!

Our oceans create some of the most difficult sporting challenges that exist on our planet today. It's only natural that we are drawn to compete there.

Enjoy the read.

—Sailor Alex Thomson

Introduction

It has long been an unwritten law of the sea, now sanctioned in international law, that if a ship is in trouble, a nearby vessel will go to its aid. Sailors obey this law unquestioningly, partly because they know that they could be the next person who needs rescuing. Even if seafarers fall into trouble through their own incompetence or because they take undue risks, other sailors know that, "There but for the grace of God go I." The sea is like that: It forces you to be humble.

That is why, when Tony Bullimore and Rafael Dinelli capsized in their yachts 1,500 miles (2,400 km) off the west coast of Australia, there was never any question of not trying to rescue them, even though no one knew for sure if Bullimore was still alive. The 4,100-ton frigate HMAS *Adelaide*, with her crew of 185 men, was duly sent off on a 3,000-mile (4,800-km) rescue mission that cost the Australian navy an estimated $5 million. Neither Bullimore nor Dinelli ever paid a penny.

The local media kicked up a storm about the burden these irresponsible yachtsmen were placing on the Australian taxpayer, and Bullimore seemed to sympathize with them. "There is something a little absurd about the tremendous cost of rescuing people who attempt difficult challenges," he told a press conference back in Perth, Australia. "I have thought about it very deeply, and I don't know whether we have the right to lean on society, communities, or countries and say, 'Well here we are, come and rescue us.' At the same time, people walk to the South Pole, sail the oceans of the world, go up as high as they can…whatever. If all these things were taken away, it would be a little like the taming of mankind."

Which really gets to the heart of the matter. For there is no doubt that the world would be a poorer place without these daring souls, ready to put their lives on the line to test the limits of mankind's capabilities. Without them, no one would have discovered America, nor gone to the moon, and we would still believe that the Earth was flat. Mankind needs risk takers in order to evolve and develop and move beyond the mundane. They drive all of us to achieve a little bit more, to realize that we can step out of our limited existences and dare to lead richer, better lives.

Dom Mee, rescued off Newfoundland, Canada, while trying to kite sail across the Atlantic was met by a similar reaction. He answered his critics by saying, "Whilst I had no intention of being a drain on the taxpayer, as indeed I haven't been on any of my previous expeditions, this one didn't work out that way. Maritime exploration is my job; I earn my living from the ocean just as our brave fishermen do. Without people making discoveries and testing new theories, we really would believe the world to be flat."

Most of the sailors whose stories are told in the following pages didn't set out to change the world. Most set out because they loved the freedom, the adventure and, above all, the sea. Some of them may have hoped for fame and glory, but many were just ordinary people who found themselves in extraordinary circumstances. Whatever their motives when they started out, when the crunch came, the sea treated them all in the same way. It is how they dealt with circumstances that makes their stories so interesting. For although these stories are all about boats and the sea, above all, they are stories about people, their motivations, their fears, and their triumphs.

Asked why sailors embark on these voyages, Sir Robin Knox-Johnston, who came to fame as the first man to sail nonstop single-handed around the world, replied: "They are competing to prove themselves and gain the personal satisfaction of facing a savage ocean and winning through. Many will be frightened near to death, but they will live with that fear and master it alone. They will push themselves past their own personal limits, and, as a result, will feel a sense of satisfaction that I can only describe as sheer ecstasy."

"Sheer ecstasy" may be a lot to ask for, but I hope these stories will provide some pleasure and, perhaps, inspire readers to imagine the impossible.

—Nic Compton

Atlantic

Grace L. Fears

Overall length
130 ft. (40 m)

Length on deck
100 ft. (30 m)

Beam
22 ft. (7 m)

Draft
10 ft. (3 m)

Displacement
200 tons

Sail area
4,900 sq. ft. (557 m²)

Interesting facts
A dory is a flat-bottomed craft, usually 15 to 22 feet (4.5 m to 6.7 m) long, with high sides angled out at about 30 degrees. The boats were once ubiquitous across the East Coast of America. One of the most successful dory builders in the United States was Simeon Lowell in Massachusetts in 1793. So seaworthy were his boats that Lowell told fishermen: "If you get caught in a storm away from your ship in a dory, lie down and ride it out because the odds that it will swamp and capsize are almost nil."

The origin of the boats' name is unknown, but it is thought it may have derived from a redfish found in Nova Scotia called the John Dory. They are also known as the Little Lady of the North Atlantic. The most famous Grand Banks schooner of all time was the Canadian vessel *Bluenose*. Launched in Lunenburg, Nova Scotia on March 26, 1921, she won the International Fishermen's Trophy back from the United States that year and remained undefeated for the next sixteen.

The fishermen of Grand Banks, a group of underwater plateaus southeast of Newfoundland, were a hardy breed, but none more so than Howard Blackburn. The valiant doryman survived Atlantic gales and blizzards by freezing his hands to his boat's oars and rowing them down to the bone. And he didn't finish there, either.

The Man Who Wouldn't Give Up

Howard Blackburn (1883)

It was just another day fishing on the Grand Banks for Howard Blackburn and Tom Welch when they headed off in their open dory on January 25, 1883. They had set sail with the schooner *Grace L. Fears* from Gloucester, Massachusetts, three days earlier and headed for the Burgeo Bank, a fishing ground 60 miles (97 km) south of Newfoundland. Once there, the schooner began unloading its complement of six 18-foot (5.4-m) dories—with their distinctive flared sides and flat bottoms—and the crews rowed off to set their lines.

For years fishermen had known about the abundant harvest in the fertile waters of the Grand Banks in the northwest Atlantic. The meeting of two currents, the cold Labrador current from the north and the warm Gulf Stream from the south, had created a rich environment for all kinds of marine life, and the waters were teeming with fish—cod and halibut, in particular. The method they used to catch the fish was a long line rigged with hundreds of hooks, which were baited and laid on the seabed by the dories. A trawl might be a mile and a half (2.4 km) long and hold 500 hooks. It took about an hour to set, and afterward the dorymen would return to the schooner, have a brew, maybe smoke a pipe, and then go back to retrieve the trawl, now heavy with fish weighing up to 400 lb. (180 kg) each.

So far so good. The only problem was that the very conditions that had created such a rich breeding ground for fish also produced unpredictable and often dramatic weather. The Grand Banks was not a place for the fainthearted.

Howard Blackburn knew the dangers. Born in Nova Scotia in 1859, he migrated to Gloucester when he was in his teens and had served as a doryman on several Grand Banks schooners before signing up with the *Grace L. Fears*. His dorymate Tom Welch, from Newfoundland, was much younger and less experienced. It was the first time the two men had worked together.

On this particular morning the wind was blowing from the southeast, so Blackburn and the other dorymen rowed their boats in that direction, allowing the wind to blow them back toward the schooner as they laid their trawls. They were barely back on board, however, when the captain told them to retrieve their gear because he thought a blizzard was about to strike. Back in their boats, the dorymen headed for the buoys that marked the farthest end of their trawls and started hauling them in. Just as Blackburn and Welch were bringing in the last hooks, the wind died away, leaving an eerie silence. Blackburn knew exactly what this meant and hurried to unhook the last few fish.

A few minutes later the wind came in from the opposite direction, stronger and colder this time and bearing snow. The dories were now downwind of the schooner and rowing straight into the blizzard, weighed down by their trawls and their catches of fish. "We were in a whirling mass of snowflakes, some of them with sharp, frozen edges that seemed to cut the face as with a knife," Blackburn later recalled. "The snow and vapor soon became so thick we could not see many lengths ahead of us. Of course, we lost sight of the schooner in the blizzard."

The two men rowed to where they thought the schooner was located, but with no sign of her and night rapidly falling, they decided to put out an anchor so that they could stop rowing. It was a bitterly cold night, and as the snow settled, it turned to ice and threatened to capsize the dory under its weight. To lighten the boat and stop the waves from

coming over the side, they jettisoned their valuable catch of fish—all except for one 20-lb. (9-kg) mackerel, which they planned to eat raw if necessary. Later, when it stopped snowing, they caught sight of the schooner's riding light and realized that they had barely made any headway at all.

By morning the ship had vanished completely and Blackburn and Welch found themselves alone, miles out at sea, in little more than a large dinghy, being lashed by the full force of an Atlantic gale.

The pull of the anchor was threatening to drag the boat under, so they decided to set an improvised sea anchor made of one of the trawl buoys. In order to secure the buoy, however, Blackburn took off his heavy-duty fisherman's mittens, which almost immediately vanished over the side. Soon Blackburn's hands began to freeze. Rather than allow them to be rendered useless, however, he had an ingenious but painful idea. He took the oars and pressed his hands around the handles tightly until he lost all feeling in them and they turned into frozen hooks. At least now, whatever else befell them, he would be able to slide his hands onto the ends of the oars and keep rowing.

The storm continued to rage, and the boat filled with water. The men spent most of the day bailing and breaking off the ice with a gobstick—a lump of wood used to kill the fish. However, by the second night Welch was beginning to weaken.

"Come, Tom, this won't do," Blackburn said, trying to reinvigorate him. "You must do your part.

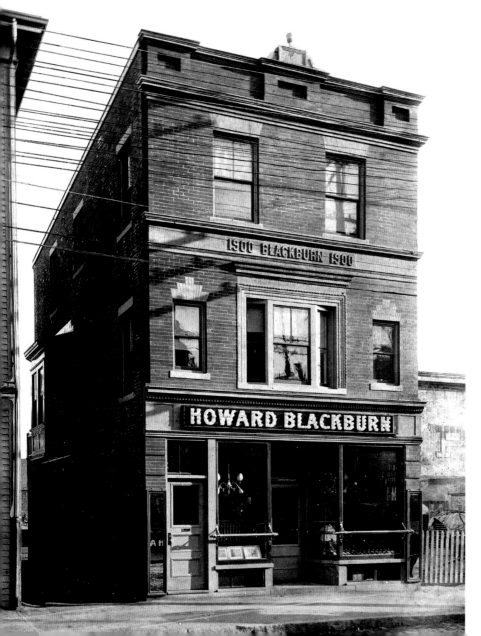

After his ordeals, the citizens of Gloucester raised money to buy a bar for Blackburn to run. He would not be landbound for long, however.

> **"The snow and vapor soon became so thick we could not see many lengths ahead of us. Of course, we lost sight of the schooner in the blizzard."**

Your hands are not frozen and beaten to pieces as mine are." "Howard, what is the use?" replied Welch, his spirit beaten by the storm. "We cannot last until morning. We might as well go first as last."

All through the night, Blackburn bailed the boat, and when he wasn't, he rocked one of the seats, willing himself to stay awake. By the time morning came, Welch was dead.

By then the wind had abated, and Blackburn rowed all day toward where he thought land must be, approximately 40 miles (65 km) away. Welch's body, slumped in the stern of the boat, acted as a constant reminder of what his possible fate would be if he gave up. That night he set the sea anchor again, and the following day he continued rowing. He finally reached land just before nightfall, and here he found shelter in an empty hut in a small, apparently deserted village called Little River.

The next morning there was still no sign of anyone, so he set off again in the dory to look for help. By now his hands were in terrible shape. "I had

hardly started on my return journey when I sensed the fact that as I rowed portions of my hands and fingers were being ground off on the oar handles," he said. "It is surprising how fast dead flesh disintegrates when rubbed hard. In a short space of time it seemed as though I was holding the oars with bones and muscles only. Soon the handles became too small for my finger bones to encircle and I had to use one hand to clamp the fingers of the other down so I could work the blades."

That evening, when he returned to Little River, a small crowd gathered to meet him. After directing them to where he had left Welch's body, he was taken

The indomitable Howard Blackburn. Despite losing all his fingers and several toes to frostbite, he went on to build his own boat and sail single-handed across the Atlantic.

The Grand Banks
schooners carried
several dories that
were sent out to lay
the lines. It was not
uncommon for the
men to be lost in
storms and fog.

into the home of the Lushman family. They treated his wounds with a mixture of flour and cod liver oil and cut off the rotten flesh. Nothing could be done to undo the damage, however, and despite the Lushmans' best efforts, he lost all his fingers, half of each thumb, several toes, and the heels of both feet.

It was five months before he was able to return to Gloucester, where he was greeted as a returning hero. Because he was unable to fish, the local people raised enough money to allow him to buy a bar, which he ran successfully for many years.

> **"In a short space of time it seemed as though I was holding the oars with bones and muscles only. Soon the handles became too small for my finger bones to encircle and I had to use one hand to clamp the fingers of the other down so I could work the blades."**

And that could have been the end of the story. Blackburn, however, was an indomitable and restless spirit. Fourteen years after his experiences on the Grand Banks, he organized an expedition to Klondike in Canada to prospect for gold, sailing there via Cape Horn. Seemingly unfazed by his disability, he built a 30-foot (9-m) sloop, the *Great Western*, which in 1899 he sailed single-handedly from Gloucester, Massachusetts, to Gloucester, in the United Kingdom, in sixty-two days. Two years later he was back, this time with a 25-foot (7.6-m) sloop of his own design, the *Grand Republic*, which he sailed single-handedly to Lisbon, setting a new record of thirty-nine days. He attempted one more crossing in 1903, in a half-decked dory, but after capsizing three times between Nova Scotia and Newfoundland, he finally admitted defeat—probably for the first time in his life. By then he had become a successful businessman and a notable philanthropist, paying back to the citizens of Gloucester what they had given him. He died in 1932 at the age of 72, a legend among the New England seafaring community.

Liberdade

Overall length
35 ft. (10.6 m)

Beam
7 ft. 6 in. (2 m)

Draft
2 ft. 6 in. (0.7 m)

Displacement
6 tons

Interesting facts
Joshua Slocum was born in
Nova Scotia on February 20,
1844, and ran away to sea at
the age of 14. He returned
home but two years later got
a job as a seaman on a full-
rigged ship headed
overseas.

In 1869 Slocum got his first
command and sailed for
thirteen years out of San
Francisco to such places as
China, Japan, and Australia.

He married Virginia Walker
in Sydney in 1871 and had
three sons and a daughter by
her. In 1882 he bought shares
in the three-masted ship
Northern Light and became
her skipper. He described
her as "the finest American
ship afloat."

His most famous voyage
was in the *Spray*, in which he
became the first person to
sail around the world. It took
him from April 24, 1895, to

June 27, 1898. The journey
catapulted him into being
known as the patron of small-
boat sailing for this.

Fittingly, the sea is the last
known whereabouts of
Slocum. His final voyage was
from Martha's Vineyard on
November 14, 1909, to South
America. He disappeared
during the journey and was
never heard from again.

Joshua Slocum is best known for being the first man to sail around the world single-handed, but long before that he had already survived a shipwreck, mutiny, and disease to make a remarkable voyage across the Caribbean.

Slocum's First Adventure

Joshua Slocum (1886)

It was the moment that every ship's master dreads. Captain Joshua Slocum and his family stood by the beach on the coast of Brazil and watched, helplessly, as their ship was pounded on the surf. For three days and three nights the seas raged, until the vessel's back was broken and she was reduced to little more than a wreck. It was the culmination of a run of bad luck that saw the Nova Scotian-born captain go from being in command of his own ship and sailing the seven seas with his wife and children to losing it all—including his beloved first wife—and being left stranded on a beach thousands of miles away from home. Yet it was at this moment of desperation that Slocum came up with a solution that would not only rescue him and his family but lay the foundation for one of the greatest stories in maritime history.

It had all started so well. For several years he carried cargo between North and South America with his wife, Virginia, and their three sons and a daughter on board—all four children were born either at aboard ship or in foreign harbors. Slocum, who had sailed the world since the age of 16 and risen to the rank of captain, sold his shares in the three-masted square-rigger *Northern Light* to buy his own ship in 1884. The vessel he chose was the 326-ton Aquidneck, which he described as "a little bark which

of all man's handiwork seemed to me the nearest to perfection of beauty." She was the largest ship he had ever owned and was evidence of his hard-earned success, despite humble beginnings. On a trip to Buenos Aires in that year, however, his wife died, leaving him to care for their four children, the youngest of which was a 4-year-old boy. Although by all accounts heartbroken, Slocum remarried two years later to his cousin Henrietta, and the family resumed its nomadic life once more.

On February 28, 1886, the *Aquidneck* set sail from New York bound for Montevideo in Uruguay with a cargo of case oil. On board were Slocum; Henrietta; Slocum's eldest son, Victor, as mate; his youngest son, Garfield; and six crew. Nine and a half weeks later they arrived in Montevideo and, after unloading the oil, took on a cargo of hay to carry north to Rio de Janeiro in Brazil. By the time they left Montevideo, however, the city was in the grips of cholera, and it took six months of waiting before they were finally allowed into Rio to unload.

While in Rio they enjoyed the sights of the city, Henrietta bought a tall hat, and aboard ship "a change of rats was made," Slocum reported. "Fleas, too." Next they loaded a cargo of flour, kerosene, tar, resin, wine, three pianos, and a steam engine and boiler, and headed farther south, down the Brazilian coast for Paranagua. There, in the dead of night, he was woken up by his wife, who had heard voices on the poop deck—the part of the boat reserved for the captain and his family while in harbor. Creeping on deck with gun in hand, he found four of his crew poised to attack him, hoping to rob him of the ship's funds. "Go forward there!" he roared. Ignoring his command, first one and then another of the mutineers attacked him, but each offender was shot down. It must have been a terrifying ordeal, but Slocum passed it off with a typical mix of bravado and wisdom. "A man will defend himself and his family to the last," he wrote, "for life is sweet, after all."

After he was acquitted of murder, Slocum rejoined the *Aquidneck* in Montevideo, where his son Victor had sailed her, and they set off for

> **"My hardest task was to come, you will believe, at the gathering of the trinkets and other purchases which the crew had made… A hat for the little boy there, a pair of boots for his mama there… all had to be destroyed!"**

Paranagua once again with a new cargo and crew. Two days out, however, one of the deck hands came down "with rigor in the spine" and they were forced to head back to harbor. They had been infected with smallpox, and there was so much fear of the disease that, rather than receiving help, the "pest-ridden ship" was told to leave harbor immediately. Several days later, after burying two sailors at sea, the *Aquidneck* was finally admitted into Montevideo and the remaining crew was taken ashore for treatment—although it was too late for Slocum's faithful chef, who died within sight of the ship. Although he and his family survived, the whole episode cost Slocum over $1,000, as well as several good crew members. "My hardest task was to come, you will believe, at the gathering of the trinkets and other purchases which the crew had made, thoughtful

of wife and child at home… A hat for the little boy there, a pair of boots for his mama there…all had to be destroyed!"

By now *Aquidneck* had a new job, shipping timber out of the Brazilian town of Guarakasava, and Slocum and his family spent a reflective Christmas in 1887. They had gone back to Montevideo and met some of the crew that had survived the smallpox, and the sight of their scarred features had affected the skipper deeply. He wasn't able to dwell on that for long,

Slocum became known as the patron of small-boat sailing.

The *Spray* was an old oyster boat on which, later in life, Slocum became the first man to sail single-handed around the world.

however; a few days later, as the *Aquidneck* sailed out of Guarakasava, she stalled while turning into the wind and started drifting toward the shore. The crew dropped an anchor, but it dragged through the thin sand, and Slocum's pride and joy was driven onto a sandbank. By the time the sea had finished with her, all he could do was sell her remains for salvage to pay off his crew.

Bereft of his ship, Slocum was left stranded on a beach with just his family and the few possessions he had managed to carry ashore. It seemed more than one man could endure.

"I had myself carried load on load," he later wrote, "but alas! I could not carry a mountain."

The easiest thing would have been to pay for their passage back to North America on another ship, but Slocum was a proud man, and the thought of returning home as castaways went against his nature. He began building a boat to sail his family home. It was a tall order, given the supplies at the family's

The coast of Brazil, by Rio, where the Slocum family spent much of their time, but also where Slocum was faced with a mutiny on board his ship.

disposal. Their funds had been depleted by the events of previous months, and they had only rudimentary tools. But they soon pulled everything together and started laying down the bare bones of a boat.

Their tool kit consisted of an ax, an adze, two saws, three drill bits, and a file, which were supplemented by a homemade square, a compass made of bamboo, and clamps constructed from guava wood. All of the timber for the boat came from either the cargo salvaged from the *Aquidneck* or it was cut straight from the jungle itself. Fastenings were also salvaged from the wreck or they were made by melting the ship's copper sheathing and casting it into nails. The washers, or "roves," on the inside were made from coins with holes punched through the middle. Rope was made from three

strands of wild vine twisted together. The sails were made by Henrietta using a salvaged sewing machine, which was swapped for an anchor once the sails were completed.

The design of the boat was an intriguing mix of cultures: The hull was an American fishing boat crossed with a Japanese sampan, while the rig took its inspiration from the junk-rigged vessels Slocum had seen during his travels in the Far East. In typical Chinese fashion the sails were fitted with bamboo battens, giving them the appearance of a strangely shaped fan. At 35 feet (10.6 m) long the Slocums' "microscopic ship" could have been a dinghy to the *Aquidneck*. Even with the addition of a tarpaulin roof over the central cabin, there was only 4 feet (1.2 m) of sitting headroom down below. As young Garfield

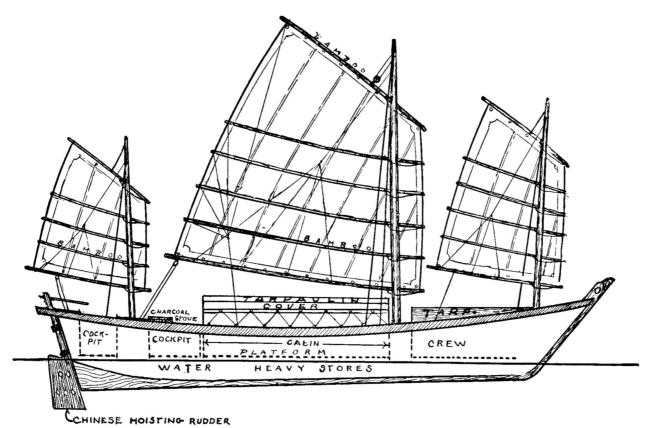

The *Liberdade* was a cross between the sampans of the Far East and the traditional American dory. It was also the easiest type of boat to build on a beach with minimal tools.

Cabin profile and sail plan of *Liberdade* as fitted for the voyage from Brazil to New York. Length, 35' 0"; Beam, 7' 6"; Depth of hold 3'; Weight 6 tons.

would later comment as he struggled to find somewhere comfortable to kneel, "Mama, this boat isn't big enough to pray in!"

On May 13, 1888, less than five months after the family were shipwrecked, their new vessel was launched and named the *Liberdade* (or Liberty) because it was the day the government gave all Brazilian slaves their freedom. She was soon loaded with stores for the voyage, including 100 lb. (45 kg) dried beef, 20 lb. (9 kg) pork, 20 lb. (9 kg) dried cod, 120 lb. (54 kg) sea biscuits, 30 lb. (13.5 kg) sugar, 25 lb. (11 kg) flour, 9 lb. (4 kg) coffee, 3 lb. (1.3 kg) tea, 200 oranges, six bunches of bananas, two bottles of honey, and a basket of yams. A musket and three machetes were also on board for good measure.

Six weeks later the *Liberdade* left Paranagua for the 5,500-mile (8,850-km) journey to Washington, D.C. Despite numerous obstacles—grounding on a reef, breaking the main mast, and enduring the attentions of an overamorous whale—the family arrived back in home waters on October 28. By then they were minor celebrities, with newspapers on both sides of the Atlantic reporting their adventures. Despite this, once back on land, Henrietta refused to return to sea.

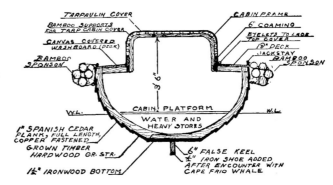

Midship Section of *Liberdade*.

For Captain Slocum it was a frustrating time: Sails were replaced by steam; and his skills were no longer required. Instead, he turned to writing, and he published a book about the voyage of the *Liberdade*. But his nomadic spirit would not let him stay landbound for long. In 1892 he acquired an old oyster boat, the *Spray*, and spent three years restoring her before setting off once again, this time alone, on another remarkable voyage: 46,000 miles (74,000 km) around the world. For both of these achievements, he is justifiably regarded as the patron of small boat sailing.

L'Hérétique

Overall length
15 ft. (4.65 m)

Beam
6 ft. (1.9 m)

Year
1952

Class
Zodiac Mk III

Designer
Pierre Debroutelle

Interesting facts
Pierre Debroutelle designed the first inflatable dinghies for the French Navy as a means of transporting torpedoes and bombs safely. After the war, Zodiac branched out into the leisure market, but it wasn't until Dr. Alain Bombard's pioneering journey that the boats' seaworthiness was fully appreciated. Made of five hermetically sealed compartments joined together by a wooden transom, the boat had a rigid keel and wooden slats for a floor. A simple, unstayed mast set a small sail, though even with leeboards attached to the side of the boat, it was impossible to sail into the wind. This type of boat was the forerunner to what nowadays is commonly known as a RIB lifeboat.

Rigid inflatable boats usually measure between 13 feet (4 m) and 23 feet (7 m) long and are often powered by outboard motors, or an inboard motor that turns a water jet. They are most commonly used as rescue craft and safety boats for sailing boats. RIBs up to 23 feet (7 m) long are sometimes used for leisure because they can be towed on a trailer behind a car, making them easily transportable.

When Dr. Alain Bombard proposed crossing the Atlantic without food or water, everyone thought he was insane. But the doctor wanted to prove a point, and as it turned out, finding food and drink was the least of his problems.

Heresy on the High Seas

Alain Bombard (1952)

Alain Bombard was working at a hospital in Boulogne in the spring of 1951 when a fire engine delivered a grim cargo: the bodies of forty-three dead or dying men. They had been on a trawler, which had missed the harbor entrance in the fog and crashed into the outer mole. They had all been wearing life jackets, but no one survived.

The incident left Bombard thinking about the number of lives lost in shipwrecks. According to his research, around 100 to 150 fishermen died in Boulogne every year, while an astonishing 200,000 people died in shipwrecks around the world—this was the 1950s, when ships and trains were still the prevalent means of long-distance transportation. A quarter of those people, he discovered, died after reaching their lifeboats, through thirst, starvation, or madness.

Bombard was convinced that many of these deaths were avoidable. His studies demonstrated that there were nearly 200 times as many living organisms in a cubic foot of water as there were in the same amount of earth. Surely there must be a good way of harvesting that source of energy. And as for dehydration, a far greater killer than hunger, his experience had shown that contrary to popular belief, drinking small amounts of saltwater would not drive a castaway insane but could sustain the human body for a limited period of time—about five days, he estimated—until an alternative was found. That alternative, he proposed, was fish juice. A fish's body is made up of 60 to 80 percent water. If one crushed them in a common fruit press, the liquid from a fish could provide a thirst-quenching and nutritious drink.

As for scurvy—traditionally another killer at sea, where natural sources of vitamin C are hard to find—Bombard began thinking about whales. They achieved all of their nutritional needs through consuming vast amounts of plankton. He therefore suggested that by trawling a fine net behind the boat, enough plankton could be collected to achieve a balanced diet.

It sounded good, but how could he prove his theories? The memory of those forty-three bodies, piled up like stringless puppets, weighed heavily on his soul. If he could only show that his ideas were indeed correct, perhaps some of those thousands of shipwrecked sailors could be saved. While spending some time on boats in the English Channel, he came up with a plan: He would sail across the Atlantic without taking any food or drink with him and live purely off the ocean. And he would do it in an inflatable boat, similar to the life rafts carried by ships. In this scenario he would realistically experience what it was like to be a castaway.

It was a pretty wild idea, and virtually everyone he spoke to tried to talk him out of doing it. He was also subjected to endless ridicule for going against virtually every known theory of survival at sea. And you have to admire his wife, Ginette, for

> **"While messing around on boats in the Channel, he came up with a plan: He would sail across the Atlantic without taking any food or drink with him and live purely off the ocean."**

allowing him to go ahead with it—especially considering that she was several months pregnant when he began his journey.

Before facing the Atlantic, he decided to make a trial run across the Mediterranean from Monaco, on

the south coast of France—where he was by now working at the Museum of Oceanography—to Gibraltar, on the south coast of Spain. Although he had crossed the English Channel to Folkestone in the United Kingdom and back in a rubber dinghy, Bombard was not a sailor. He was therefore fortunate, while in Monaco, to meet an Englishman, Jack Palmer, who was an accomplished navigator. Palmer volunteered to join him on the journey.

His old friend Jean van Hemsbergen, who had accompanied him on several of his English Channel jaunts, offered to come along, too, but backed out when he saw the size of Bombard's craft. This was unfortunate because van Hemsbergen was a radio

Palmer, however, who hung up his life jacket during the long stopover in Tangiers and allowed the doctor to continue with his adventure alone.

On August 13 Bombard set off alone from Tangiers to begin the next stage of his odyssey. Although he would miss the likeable Englishman and the helpful Dutchman, his main concern at this point was how to navigate his craft, because the doctor was not a sailor. It didn't take him long, however, to master the basics of navigation. By the third day out at sea, he was already learning to use a sextant. After a stopover in Casablanca, he made his first ocean crossing to the Canary Islands, arriving there after eleven days, just in time to hear some important news: He had a baby daughter.

After a quick trip back to Paris to visit his newborn, he finally set off from Las Palmas on October 19 to begin the most audacious part of his journey: across the Atlantic to whatever island the winds and currents—assisted by as much steerage as his rudimentary sail and rudder afforded—would carry him. He left with no food supplies, clothing, tools, or bedding. Even if he had been able to use the radio, it's unlikely that it would have been effective from such a low platform. The only backup he had was a first-aid kit and a few survival rations of food and drink, both of which were sealed and hidden in the bowels of the boat in case of an emergency.

Bombard believed his theories could save thousands of shipwrecked sailors. His research showed that 200,000 people a year died at sea—a quarter of them in life rafts.

In order to prove that survival was possible by a "normal" castaway, Bombard made no major modifications to his inflatable boat and carried no special equipment with him.

expert and would have kept them in touch with the outside world. The best Bombard and Palmer could do in Morse code was "Yes," "No," and "SOS," and they certainly wouldn't know how to fix the radio if it failed.

A favorable wind was blowing when the two self-styled castaways set off from Monaco on the 15-foot (4.65-m) *L'Hérétique* on May 26, 1952. But navigating an inflatable dinghy that will sail only off the wind isn't an exact science, so it isn't surprising that they ended up in Minorca, one of the Balearic Islands, rather than Gibraltar. From Minorca they took a ship to Tangiers, Morocco, rather than try to sail against the prevailing winds. But their seventeen-day adventure, including ten days of drinking seawater, proved that the theory worked and, although Bombard had to lance an abscess in his gum with a sterilized knife, neither of them suffered from any serious health problems. The trip was enough for

Unable to catch enough fish in sufficient quantity to make his juice, he drank straight from the sea for the first six days. In fact, he became something of a connoisseur of seawater. He wrote in his diary: "Atlantic water tastes absolutely delicious compared with that of the Mediterranean. Much less salty and quenches my thirst perfectly."

Still acting out his castaway part, which was becoming increasingly real, he made a makeshift

his own catch, most mornings he would find several flying fish that had landed on the boat during the night, which provided a fine breakfast. And by towing a net behind the boat for a couple of hours, he was able to keep up his self-imposed regime of swallowing two spoonfuls of plankton sludge every day—the oceangoing equivalent of vitamin tablets. He celebrated his twenty-eighth birthday by catching a shearwater bird on the end of his fishing line, which he plucked and ate raw. Even that tasted like fish.

> **"Atlantic water tastes absolutely delicious compared with that of the Mediterranean. Much less salty and quenches my thirst perfectly."**

In fact, the most troublesome part of the whole crossing was the navigation. Nine days out his watch stopped working, which meant

harpoon by lashing his knife onto the end of an oar. On the sixth day he caught a dorado. It was a double bounty: Not only was it big enough to juice, but one of the bones inside the gills made a natural hook that Bombard could attach to the end of his fishing line. From then on, he never went hungry. In addition to

he was unable to work out his line of longitude. By measuring the angle of the sun at its highest point above the horizon, however, he could work out how far above the equator he was located and therefore which islands he was likely to hit first. But when? As days and then weeks passed, he was buffeted by sharks, swordfish, and an amorous whale that he named Amelia, but there was still no sight of land. Finally, after nearly eight weeks at sea, a British ship passed and gave him his position: He was 600 miles (965 km) farther away than he had estimated! Resisting the temptation to catch a lift, he carried on for another two weeks on *L'Hérétique* before finally landing in Barbados on December 23.

Dr. Bombard proved his point: Man could survive at sea by living off what the elements provided, and at no point had he broken into his emergency supplies. However, his experiment was achieved with some personal cost. By the time he reached Barbados, he had lost 55 lb. (25 kg) and was seriously anemic. His whole body was covered in a rash, and he had lost all his toenails. But, as he put it, "I had got there."

Perhaps it's not a surprise that Bombard's techniques for survival did not meet with immediate approval. People were, however, impressed with the seaworthiness of his little inflatable dinghy, and Zodiac, the manufacturers of the dinghy, soon became the dominant brand in France and around the world. The doctor was not rewarded for the success of the boat. Instead, he lent his name to a line of life rafts, which were frequently used by the French Navy. He went on to found a marine research laboratory in St. Malo and, in 1981, was invited to join the government as Secretary of State to the Minister for the Environment. And, this time, there was no more talk of heresy.

His voyage made Bombard a media celebrity and later led to a role in the French government.

Teignmouth Electron

Length overall
41 ft. (12.5 m)

Waterline length
38 ft. (11.5 m)

Beam
22 ft. (6.7 m)

Sail area
600 sq. ft. (55.7 m²)

Distance sailed
16,591 miles (26,700 km)

Time
243 days

Interesting facts
Crowhurst's Golden Globe rivals were: Robin Knox-Johnston on Suhaili (313 days); Bernard Moitessier on Joshua (retired); Chay Blyth on Dytiscus (retired); John Ridgeway on English Rose (retired); Bill King on Galway Blazer (retired after capsize); Nigel Tetley on Victress (boat sank); Loïck Fougeron on Captain Brown (retired after knock down); and Alex Carooze on Gancia American, (retired with ill health).

The rules of the Golden Globe race stated that competitors should start from any British port between June 1 and October 31, 1968. The route was around the world via the three Capes (Good Hope, Leeuwin, and Horn), without stopping and without assistance. The Golden Globe itself would be awarded to the first boat to return to its starting point, while a prize of $12,000 (£5000) would be awarded to the fastest boat on elapsed time. The race was different than others because it was open to all, instead of requiring the sailors to prove their ability beforehand.

Donald Crowhurst was just three days out of the harbor in Teignmouth when he realized that his boat was unfit for the round-the-world race he had entered. Faced with certain bankruptcy if he turned back, he devised a cunning plan to save himself. Soon he was caught in a web of deceit with only one way out.

Secrets and Lies

Donald Crowhurst (1968)

Donald Crowhurst had a grand vision when he entered the *Sunday Times* Golden Globe Race in autumn 1968: To be the first man to sail single-handed around the world without stopping and, in so doing, promote his electronics company, Electron Utilisation. By sailing a modern three-hulled boat, a trimaran, and fitting it with all of his latest high-tech inventions, he would not only gain an advantage over his competitors, he would also prove the efficacy of his equipment and be able to sell it once he completed his voyage. It was a fantastic marketing opportunity, and in the process he hoped to win the Golden Globe trophy as the first man home and scoop the $12,000 (£5,000) prize for the fastest circumnavigation.

And Crowhurst had plenty of wizardly ideas. Apart from the radio direction finder, which his company was already manufacturing, he devised an ingenious system of automated devices that were linked to a central "computer" to control the boat. Stress detectors on the rigging would warn of excess pressure on the mast, while any sudden change in wind speed would be picked up by the machine, which would automatically ease the sails. To guard against a capsize, Crowhurst proposed fitting electrodes to the trimaran's floats that, when immersed for a period of time, would inflate a rubber buoyancy bag at the top of the mast to prevent the boat from inverting. A pair of pumps connected to the floats by a system of pipes would then allow the upended float to be filled with water to right the vessel.

It all sounded very impressive, and Crowhurst managed to make it sound plausible, but the truth was very far from the picture he presented to the outside world. His business was actually on the verge of collapse, and by the time he had managed to raise the money for his circumnavigation, time was already running out. *Teignmouth Electron*, his modified Victress trimaran, was launched on September 23 on England's east coast. From the outset her performance was disappointing, and with crew changes and bad weather it took him thirteen days to sail her around the coast to Teignmouth.

By the time he set off from the United Kingdom on October 31, the latest possible date to qualify for the race, both the boat and its skipper were hopelessly unprepared. Boxes of supplies were randomly piled up below deck, while essential spare parts had been left ashore. His rigging was a mess of tangled lines, and most of his sails had not been out of their bags until a few hours before his departure. As for his famous computer, it was still just several boxes of electronic parts waiting to be assembled. And most of the neatly labeled wiring that had so impressed visitors on the boat led to nowhere.

Three days out of Teignmouth, while Crowhurst was still in sight of land, the inevitable problems started to develop. The yacht's self-steering gear began shedding screws, and because most of his spare parts were in England, he had to cannibalize other fittings to fix it. He then discovered that one of the floats was filling up with water. Unable to find the hose to connect to the pump, he had to bail it out with a bucket and sponge. It was manageable in the variable weather he was encountering at that point but would be virtually impossible once he got into the continuous surf of the Southern Ocean.

By the end of the second week, there was so much wrong with the boat that Crowhurst put his chances of survival at "not better than 50-50." In addition, his progress south was depressingly slow, mostly because of the yacht's seeming inability to sail at less than 60 degrees into the wind. It looked more and more unlikely that he would win either prize. None of his anticapsize measures had been activated, despite the fact that he rated his chances of capsizing as high as six out of ten. For the first time, he seriously considered withdrawing from the race. However, he had signed an agreement with his sponsor whereby if the journey failed, he would forfeit the boat. On the other hand, if he pulled out, he would have to cope with the humiliation of defeat and face certain bankruptcy.

Then, in the third week, everything changed. Three of his competitors opted out with various health or technical problems, and the race was wide open again. By December 10 Crowhurst was reporting his fastest run to date: 243 miles (390 km) in one day—a new world record for a single-hander. Despite skepticism from the race chairman, Francis Chichester, the announcement made headline news back in the United Kingdom. Crowhurst's daily progress continued to improve until the end of January, when he was reported to be entering the Indian Ocean. There were no communications from the yacht for nearly three months, leading to feverish speculation in the media about the location of the *Teignmouth Electron*. Some people suggested that she might have sunk, but most assumed that her power supply or radio had simply broken down.

On April 10 Crowhurst's U.K. press agent received a momentous message: "HEADING DIGGER RAMREZ." It also reported a broken log—the instrument that measures the speed of the boat—

and asked for an update on the race. The message suggested that *Teignmouth Electron* was approaching Cape Horn—Diego Ramirez is a small island off the cape—and was not only still in the running but on track to win the prize for fastest circumnavigation. By then only two other boats were left in the race: Robin Knox-Johnston, who was just twelve days away from claiming the Golden Globe, and Nigel Tetley, who was racing up the Atlantic in a trimaran the same design as *Teignmouth Electron*, hoping to win the elapsed-time prize.

When Tetley heard that Crowhurst was back in contention, he pulled out all the stops in a desperate last-ditch effort to better his time. However, as he piled on the pressure, his trimaran's condition deteriorated, and fighting through a storm off the

> He had signed an agreement with his sponsor whereby if the journey failed, he would forfeit the boat. On the other hand, if he pulled out, he would have to cope with the humiliation of defeat and face certain bankruptcy.

Azores, she broke up and sank. Tetley was forced to escape to his life raft and watch his dreams sink to the bottom of the ocean.

Crowhurst now seemed certain to win the elapsed-time prize, and a welcome committee convened in Teignmouth to prepare for his arrival. Chichester was back on the warpath, demanding to see documentation. However, there was a mood of celebration—especially for Crowhurst's wife, Clare, and their two young children, who hadn't seen their father for eight months.

The party never happened. On July 10 *Teignmouth Electron* was discovered drifting in the mid-Atlantic. There was no sign of her skipper, but there were two sets of logs on board, which revealed one of the most bizarre tales in yachting history.

After deciding that his boat wasn't safe to cross the Southern Ocean and unwilling to face the consequences of defeat, Crowhurst opted for deception on a grand

Crowhurst had to scramble to untangle the rigging on *Teignmouth Electron*, just hours before the deadline for the Golden Globe expired.

scale. He worked out a probable route around the world with fast but realistic speeds and on December 6 started reporting false positions. On the day he claimed his record-breaking 243-mile (390-km) run, he had actually sailed just 170 miles (273 km)—a respectable distance, but nowhere near a record. He continued giving fake positions all the way down the Atlantic until, by the time he reached the coast of Brazil, he was claiming to be several hundred miles ahead of his actual location.

But his deception went beyond reporting false positions. Crowhurst knew that when he returned to the United Kingdom, his navigation records would be examined by the race committee, so he started writing two ship's logs: One recorded his fake positions and the other tracked his real positions. To make the fake log look authentic, he had to work out artificial sextant calculations working backward from his invented daily positions, a complex mathematical procedure considerably more difficult than taking a real sight. And he had to do it every day of his fictional voyage. Because a ship's log also includes observations of weather conditions and any other significant happenings on that day, Crowhurst had to listen to hours of special shipping bulletins broadcast in Morse code, scribbling down any information that related to his supposed location. By the end of the voyage, he had written approximately 100,000 words of notes.

On January 19, when Crowhurst reported that he was 100 miles (160 km) southeast of Gough Island, part of the South Atlantic and Subantarctic Islands and well into the Southern Ocean, he was more than 2,000 miles (3,200 km) farther back, just east of Rio de Janeiro. At this point, realizing that the position of his radio signal would give him away, he stopped transmitting. For nearly three months, while the rest of the world thought he was sailing around the Southern Ocean and unable to communicate, he maintained complete radio silence and never left the southern Atlantic. He made only one landfall, on March 6, when he stopped at Rio Salado in Argentina to repair the damage to one of his floats—an act that would have eliminated him from the race.

Crowhurst reached his most southerly point, just north of the Falkland Islands on March 29, and he enjoyed some genuine Southern Ocean sailing for a couple of days before he started to head back up the Atlantic. By the time he broke radio silence on April 10, claiming to be approaching Cape Horn, he was actually three quarters of the way up the Argentine coast. Although the position he gave in his "HEADING DIGGER RAMREZ" message was taken to mean that he had a two-week advantage over Tetley, it seems unlikely that Crowhurst wanted to win the race at this stage. As the winner, his log books would come under close scrutiny and, despite his

elaborate fake entries, the hoax stood a good chance of being exposed. By coming in second, however, he would save face, keep his boat, and, crucially, not be examined too closely.

He planned to return to his reported position on May 4 at a point approximately 700 miles (1,120 km) east of Buenos Aires—still far enough away from the finish to make it a real race for first place. However, once Tetley's boat had sunk, *Teignmouth Electron* was guaranteed victory in the elapsed-time race. Ironically, it was the last thing he wanted at that point.

In the heat of the Doldrums, Crowhurst's behavior became increasingly irrational. Apparently obsessed with making radio contact with Clare, he spent two weeks unsuccessfully soldering electronic components to make a transmitter—all of his other radios were broken except one for sending and receiving telegrams. Then, as he entered the North Atlantic, passing the Canary Islands to the east, he spent a week writing a 25,000-word treatise about God, mathematics, and his "theory of progress." After working through his arguments, he concluded:

> *"Now is revealed the true*
> *nature and purpose and power*
> *of the game offence I am*
> *I am what I am and I*
> *See the nature of my offence!"*

It was, almost, a confession. And then:

> *"It is finished*
> *It is finished*
> *IT IS THE MERCY!"*

The exact circumstances are not known, but it is generally accepted that Crowhurst probably threw himself overboard, possibly taking with him a fourth log book. His body was never found.

As the news came in that *Teignmouth Electron* was found empty, concern immediately focused on Clare and the children. The *Sunday Times* donated $12,000 (£5,000) for their welfare, and Robin Knox-Johnston—who was the only skipper to complete the race and therefore awarded the elapsed-time prize as well as the Golden Globe—donated his winnings to the family. It wasn't until several weeks later, when Crowhurst's logs were handed over, that the truth emerged and caused a national sensation. Both the *Sunday Times* and Knox-Johnston, however, stuck with their decisions. As the race winner put it: "None of us should judge him too harshly."

History was less kind. Several books and films were produced based on Crowhurst's story— including the 2006 docudrama *Deep Water*—and he is invariably portrayed as a mad genius, too proud to admit his mistake. Several of his inventions, however, have been developed and are used on luxury yachts, proving that there was some method behind his madness.

The trimaran was taken to Jamaica and sailed for several years in the Caribbean before being abandoned on the Cayman Islands.

Grimalkin

Overall length
30 ft. 3 in. (9.2 m)

Waterline length
24 ft. 9 in. (7.5 m)

Draft
6 ft. (1.8 m)

Beam
10 ft. 3 in. (3 m)

Displacement
8 tons

Designer
Ron Holland

Class
Half-tonner

Interesting facts
The Fastnet Race was started in 1925 by British yachtsman Weston Martyr. Its 608-mile (978-km) course starts off the Isle of Wight, rounds the Fastnet Rock off the south coast of Ireland, and finishes

in Plymouth, Cornwall. The first boat to win the race was the legendary Le Havre pilot cutter *Jolie Brise*, and since then a string of famous yachts have vied for victory. Known as one of the toughest races in the world, it formed part of the Admiral's Cup series from 1957 to 1999. After the 1979 disaster, the event hit the headlines again in 1985 when pop star Simon Le Bon's yacht *Drum* was capsized, trapping

the crew in the hull for 20 minutes until they were rescued by the Royal Navy.

The Fastnet Rock lighthouse is known as the teardrop of Ireland, because it was emigrants' last view of Ireland when they were leaving for America. It is 177 feet (54 m) high and sends out a flash of white light every six seconds. If there is fog, it sends a signal of four blasts every sixty seconds.

The 1979 Fastnet race will always be remembered as the most fatal in yachting history. Yet behind the headlines, each of the competing 303 yachts had a personal tale of courage, fortitude, and sometimes failure. This is one of those stories.

The Day of Reckoning

David Sheahan (1979)

The crew members of *Grimalkin* were in high spirits as they headed out of the Hamble River, near Southampton, in the United Kingdom on August 11, 1979. They were about to start off on the famous Fastnet race: 608 miles (978 km) along the south coast of England, across the Irish Sea to the Fastnet Rock, and then back to Plymouth in Devon. The six men were assigned their jobs, and the boat was meticulously well prepared for the journey, which would normally take about five or six days, depending on the weather. The forecast predicted southwesterly winds of 17 to 27 knots, possibly rising to 35 knots once they reached the rock. It would make for a fast, exciting run, but nothing too scary. As they approached the starting line off the Royal Yacht Squadron, they sang songs and joked loudly with each other. Then, *bang*! The start cannon was fired, and they were off.

It was a record year for the 54-year-old race. The entrants included some big names, such as the former British prime minister Edward Heath on *Morning Cloud*. At 30 feet (9 m), *Grimalkin* was one of the smaller boats and was therefore placed in Class V, which had fifty-eight entries and was the first to start. Designed by Ron Holland, one of the most successful designers of the time, and built by the legendary Camper & Nicholsons boatyard, the yacht had an impeccable pedigree. Although he was a relative newcomer to ocean racing, her owner, David Sheahan, had an accountant's eye for detail that would have shamed many of the veterans in the race. In addition to the inflatable life raft, flares, and life jackets specified by the race rules, *Grimalkin* carried three very high frequency radios—two fixed and one portable—and she was fitted with jackwires along her deck and in the cockpit, which the crew could clip on to as they moved around the boat.

The wind blew steadily from the southwest for the first two days at around 10 to 15 knots—slightly less than forecasted—until, on the morning of August 13, it died and was replaced by a stiff northeasterly breeze. *Grimalkin* shot past Land's End in Cornwall, under spinnaker making a healthy 8 knots, and her crew felt exhilarated as they left the land behind them and headed out into the open sea. Within a few hours that feeling changed to foreboding as the clouds stacked up in the west and French radio stations started predicting 60-knot winds—in other words, a full-fledged storm. The British meteorological office, however, was still insisting on 22 to 27 knots, with local gales of up to 40 knots.

By 11:00 P.M. *Grimalkin* was sailing under storm jib alone and making 6 knots on her northwesterly course, still doggedly trying to round the Fastnet Rock. Although none of her crew knew it at the time,

it was a course that would take *Grimalkin* into the most ferocious part of the storm. As they huddled together in the cockpit, they were drenched by an almost constant avalanche of rain and spray.

As the wind steadily increased and the crew were forced to lower even the small storm jib, Sheahan realized that the situation had changed from racing to survival. They gave up trying to reach the rock and turned the boat downwind so that she ran with the waves rather than fighting against them. Their race was over. Yet even under bare poles, the yacht surfed down the waves at an alarming speed, at one point reaching 12 knots—a speed she would struggle to achieve under full sail even in perfect conditions.

The wind was up to 60 knots at this point, and mountainous 30-foot (9-m)-high waves were sweeping *Grimalkin* along as if she were an oversized

football, to be thrown unceremoniously from wave to wave. Most dangerous were the breaking waves, which created areas of low buoyancy into which the yacht could fall. As she skewed sideways, the wave picked up her keel and threw her sideways. It was like having a very wet rug pulled out from under your feet, while your head was simultaneously being clobbered with a large bat. The yacht was flattened by the waves six times, and each time, her crew was thrown into the water, only to be caught on the boat's guardrails as she came back up, or dragged along through the water by their safety harnesses as the yacht sped down the next wave.

At first light Sheahan and his son Matthew decided to go down below and try to sort out some of the debris, when they heard an ominous sound. "I heard this thunderous roar, a bit like I imagine an

Camargue, above, was one of twenty-four boats abandoned in the Fastnet race, after the yacht was repeatedly capsized and her crew were washed overboard.

Four of the six crew on another competing boat, *Ariadne*, died—two of them while trying to climb out of their life raft to a ship that had come to rescue them.

avalanche would sound," Matthew later told a BBC reporter. "I glanced up through the window and saw this absolutely monstrous wave that was breaking and rolling down like a huge bit of Hawaiian surf. Within seconds it had hit, and we rolled over. The boat eventually came up the right way, but my father had

by his own lifeline and was struggling to come up for air. Suddenly the mast broke, and free of its weight, the yacht righted herself. Matthew was catapulted back into the cockpit. The rest of the crew were either lying in the cockpit or hanging in the water by their lifelines. Only his father was missing.

> **"As I stood up and looked upwind, I could see a body facedown in the water. We were drifting away from it. There was absolutely no question in my mind it was my father."**

"As I stood up and looked upwind, I could see a body facedown in the water. We were drifting away from it. There was absolutely no question in my mind it

been concussed by some of the debris that was down below and wasn't in a good state."

They clambered back on deck, only to be hit by another massive wave. Once again *Grimalkin* went over, only this time she kept going until she was almost upside down and stayed there. Concussed and unable to climb free, Sheahan was trapped under the water inside the cockpit. A crew member cut his lifeline to free him, but Sheahan had already lost the fight. Meanwhile, Matthew was dragged underwater

was my father. The worst thing was that he was upwind of the boat, and the boat was drifting downwind. Had it been the other way round, we could have got the life raft or something to go downwind and help pick him up. But upwind in those conditions: impossible."

Matthew's father was never seen again.

Grimalkin was now half full of water, wallowing in the 30- to 40-foot (9- to 12-m)- waves. Two crew, Gerry Winks and Nick Ward had collapsed in the

himself of the rigging and climbed back on board. Gerry Winks was still in the water, so Ward grabbed Winks' harness and, using a sail winch, inched him back on board. Ward pumped the water out of his lungs and got him breathing again, but not for long. Winks whispered a message for his wife and died soon after.

Ward was now alone on a sinking boat, with no life raft, no functioning radio, and a dead crewmate lying next to him. His first priority was to try and stop the boat from sinking, so he went below and started bailing out water. He bailed all day, taking short naps every hour or so. By afternoon the wind began to subside and the sea became less fierce. At the end of the afternoon, he managed to attract the attention of a passing yacht, which radioed for help. As dusk fell, a helicopter appeared from the east and hovered over him, first picking up Winks's body, then winching Ward up to safety. His ordeal was over.

Back on shore he learned what had happened to the rest of the fleet. Out of 303 starters, twenty-four boats had been abandoned, 136 crew had been rescued, and fifteen people had died. It was the worst disaster in yachting history. In the following months there was a close examination of the events by race officials and the yachting media. The weather forecasting methods were under scrutiny, as well as the designs of boats that many felt had become too acutely tuned to class rules at the expense of safety.

But a great lesson had emerged: In such emergencies crews should stay with their boats for as long as possible before taking to their life rafts. Out of the boats that were abandoned, only five sank, while the rest were found damaged but still floating. Of the people that died, seven were lost in life rafts that either fell apart or capsized after they had abandoned ship. The call thereafter became: "Always step up into a life raft, never down."

As for the abandoned shipmate, Ward didn't seem to bear a grudge against his colleagues and joined Matthew Sheahan on a trip to Ireland to recover the stricken *Grimalkin*. They found her in the village of Baltimore and prepared her to sail again. Far from being turned off from sailing, Matthew continued to race the yacht and eventually became the racing and technical editor of *Yachting World* magazine. Nick Ward recently wrote a book about the 1979 Fastnet race, giving his side of an extraordinary story.

cockpit, both unconscious and buried under broken rigging. The three remaining crew members decided to abandon ship. They pulled out the life raft, tied it to the side of the boat, and inflated it. At 8:00 A.M. they climbed into the raft and cast off. It was an act for which they would receive widespread criticism—not only for abandoning their two crewmates but also for leaving their ship while it was still afloat. At the time, they felt they had no other choice.

Being in the life raft was even more terrifying than being on the boat, because the little rubber bubble was buffeted by the winds. Matthew later compared the experience to "being in a toddler's paddling pool and being thrown into serious, serious weather." The three men spent several hours being spun around the waves until a helicopter came and plucked them out of the water and took them to the Royal Navy Air Station at Culdrose in Cornwall.

Meanwhile, back on *Grimalkin*, another wave had thrown the boat on its side again and pitched the two remaining crew members into the water. Nick Ward woke up with his head underwater, banging against the side of the hull. He struggled to clear

Enza

Length
92 ft. (28 m)

Beam
43 ft. (13 m)

Draft
13 ft. (4 m)

Displacement
14 tons

Sail area
1,076 sq. ft. (100 m²)

Designer
Nigel Irens

Launched
1994

Interesting facts
When she was launched in 1984, *Enza* (then named *Formule TAG*) was the second largest pre-preg composite structure in the world. The following year, she won the Monaco to New York race with Canadian skipper Mike Birch. In 1985 she set a new 24-hour sailing record of 518 miles (833.6 km), i.e. 21.6 knots, during the Quebec to St. Malo race. Her record would remain unbroken for nine years. Enza's early *success* helped launch the career of her designer, Nigel Irens, who went on to produce Ellen MacArthur's trimaran *B&Q*, in which she set a new solo world record in 2005.

Starting off life at 80 feet (24 m) long, *Enza* has been lengthened, shortened, and relengthened no fewer than five times and had six names. She is currently reincarnated as Tony Bullimore's *Doha 2006*, having grown to 102 feet (31 m). In May 2007 he tried to sail nonstop and solo around the world in under seventy days. She is the largest monohull in which anyone has ever attempted this challenge.

Phileas Fogg proved that it could be done by train and steamer,
but could a yacht really sail around the world in less than eighty days?
As the twentieth century came to a close, there were a few committed souls
who believed it could be done—and the Jules Verne Trophy was born.

Children of Fogg

Robin Knox-Johnston & Peter Blake (1994)

Around the world in eighty days? Impossible! More than a century after Jules Verne's classic tale, the idea seemed as preposterous as ever—except that whereas in Verne's story the defining mode of transport was train and passenger ship, this time the suggestion was that it could be done in a small yacht. The prize? A trophy in the French author's name. The Jules Verne Trophy was devised in 1990 to beat the record of 109 days set during the first edition of the Vendée Globe race. That record was achieved single-handed and on a monohull craft, and there was a widespread belief that it could be considerably improved by a crewed multihull. The Jules Verne Trophy was therefore offered as a prize to the first boat to sail around the world in under eighty days. The rules were simple: The boats had to start and finish on an imaginary line between the island of Ouessant in Brittany and the Lizard in Cornwall and sail via the Cape of Good Hope, Cape Leeuwin, and Cape Horn nonstop and without outside assistance.

British sailing legend Robin Knox-Johnston teamed up with New Zealand legend-in-the-making Peter Blake for the first attempt in 1993. Their steed was the catamaran *Formule Tag*, renamed *Enza*, which was by then nearly ten years old and modified but already a past holder of the twenty-four-hour speed record. Their official opposition was French sailing

hero Bruno Peyron, with his catamaran *Commodore Explorer*, who a year earlier had astonished everyone by crossing the Atlantic in just nine days. Their unofficial opposition was French maverick Olivier de Kersauson and his trimaran *Charal*. He refused to play by the Jules Verne rules but was determined to snatch the record from under their noses all the same.

As a sign of defiance, de Kersauson left nine days before everyone else, thereby assuring himself a head start. His jumpstart would become futile, though, if he missed the right weather window, because what mattered was the total elapsed time, not the order of finishing. Following their weather router's advice, the *Enza* team crossed the starting line at 5:51 A.M. on January 31, followed six hours later by *Commodore*. As they headed down the Atlantic, they received conflicting information about de Kersauson's progress and deduced that he was sending out false positions to confuse the competition. When *Charal* eventually retired after hitting ice after twenty-three days at sea, de Kersauson and his crew were several hundred miles short of their claimed location.

Meanwhile, *Enza* and *Commodore* were locked in a gladiatorial struggle in the Southern Ocean, with the British–New Zealand team slowly closing the gap that opened up between them and the French boat on the way down the Atlantic. On February 26, however,

Launched as *Formule Tag* in 1984, the boat has been lengthened or shortened at least five times and had six names. Her most famous guise was as the record-breaking *Enza*, with Peter Blake and Robin Knox-Johnston on board.

Enza was also struck by a floating object and, with the front section of the boat flooding, was forced to retire. *Commodore* was left to finish the attempt on her own and, thanks to a lucky weather break at the very end of the course, made it home in 79 days, 6 hours, and 15 minutes to win the Jules Verne Trophy.

A year later Knox-Johnston and Blake were back, and their adversary this time was none other than the mercurial de Kersauson. Although the French sailor was still boycotting the Jules Verne organization, de Kersauson wanted to beat Peyron's record and challenged his former rivals to a "race within a race," which ensured that both boats would be pushed to their limits every inch of the way. Knox-Johnston and Blake had made considerable changes to *Enza* by then, extending the stern by 5 feet (1.5 m) and the bow by 2 feet (0.6 m) and remodeling the underbody to suit her new length of 92 feet (28 m)—making her the largest racing catamaran in the world at that time. De Kersauson also made changes to *Charal*, including finding new sponsors, and she reemerged a few days before the race as *Lyonnaise des Eaux-Dumez*.

As their paths crisscrossed down the Atlantic after the January 16 start, the two boats seemed well matched for the contest ahead. After just five days at

sea, however, *Enza* gave a little taste of what was to come by tearing across 520.9 miles (838.3 km) of water in twenty-four hours, setting a new world record. A few weeks later, as she stormed across the Southern Ocean, the catamaran built up what seemed to be an unassailable lead, at one point putting nearly 1,500 miles (2,414 km) between herself and her

On the eighth roll the boat stayed inverted and water started gushing through the air vent, slowly flooding the cabin. There was only one thing to do. Mee set off his EPIRB and his Personal Locator Beacon (PLB) and opened the hatch. A wall of water knocked the breath out of him, and he had to suppress his panic as he became tangled in ropes and struggled to reach the surface.

Once outside, he was greeted by a desolate scene. The wind was screeching over the blue-and-yellow upturned hull of *Little Murka* as she rose up to the top of 50-foot (15-m) waves and came tumbling down the other side in a cascade of foam. Both sky and sea were gray, featureless, and infinite. Both man and boat suddenly seemed very insignificant in the face of this vast, oblivious desert.

Mee dragged himself up on to the bottom of the boat and lay spread-eagled, clinging onto his trusted friend for dear life. It was close to freezing, and he knew he could easily slip into unconsciousness and slide into the water for good. He started to pray. "I believe in God," he wrote, "but I don't believe God can help those who don't show their faith through their actions—and I'm not talking about

Dom Mee and his team prepare to transport *Little Murka* to start the ocean crossing.

going to church on summer Sunday mornings. If prayers were to protect me, I would have to do everything possible to make the miracle happen."

He clung on to the bottom of the boat for five hours while the storm raged around him, until a particularly massive wave lifted the boat "halfway to heaven" before dumping her back in the trough—the right side up. It was the miracle Mee had wanted. He clambered back on board, and using every bit of line he could find, he improvised a sea anchor. With *Little Murka* tethered and headed into the wind again, he starting bailing, using the only container he could find: his grab bag. It was tedious, exhausting work, but at least it kept him moving. Once the cabin was dry, he went inside and braced himself against the onset of hypothermia. He knew he was in for a long wait. To keep himself going, he thought of all the people in the world that made his life worthwhile: his family, his friends, the Kite Quest team, and Queen Elizabeth and Prince Philip, whom he had met and who were following his progress.

Back on shore the Falmouth Coast Guard had received the signal from *Little Murka*'s EPIRB and had contacted the Joint Rescue Coordination Center in Halifax. The center then broadcast a Maritime Assistance Request to all ships in the area and sent out a Hercules airplane, Rescue 313, to search for

> He clung on to the bottom of the boat for five hours while the storm raged around him, until a particularly massive wave lifted the boat "halfway to heaven" before dumping her back in the trough—the right way up.

the hapless sailor. Once they received the signal from Mee's PLB, they knew that he was probably in the water and that his life was in immediate peril. The search was intensified. "Dom is in the worst possible place he could be in the North Atlantic," the duty watchman at Halifax informed Mee's shore crew: "It could take some time to get to him. He is

in a massive storm with 50–60 knot winds and experiencing mountainous swell. However, we will do our best."

Even with modern electronic safety equipment, finding a 14-foot (4-m) boat amid 50-foot (15-m) waves in a huge ocean is like finding a needle in a haystack. One minute it is in plain view on the crest of a wave; the next minute it's lost in the trough and, unless you happen to be looking at the right moment, you can miss it altogether. Eventually, however, Rescue 313 located *Little Murka* and, flying low over the foam-streaked waves, managed to drop an emergency pack with life raft, food, and radios. Next on the scene was the container ship *Berge Nord*, which responded to the call for assistance—as all sea vessels are obliged to do by law—and at 3:00 A.M. was in the

area waiting for daybreak to locate *Little Murka*. By then, however, the Canadian Coast Guard had sent out its own ship, the CGV *Cygnus*, with a crew of twenty, to find and rescue the "mad Brit." At 8:30 A.M. on September 26, twenty-four hours after Mee had capsized, a RIB was launched from *Cygnus* and he was transferred to the coast guard ship. But the Atlantic wasn't finished with him yet. After Dom was rescued, *Little Murka* was tethered behind *Cygnus* to be towed back to Canada. The following day, however, the tow rope snapped and *Little Murka* was abandoned. It was a bitter blow for the British adventurer coming on this day, of all days, his birthday. Not to be defeated, the little boat continued her voyage on her own and a year later she washed up in Ireland and is now safe with Dom in Devon.

The dream of kite sailing across the Atlantic didn't end there. In May 2006 the French sailor Manu Bertin became the first person to complete the crossing on a kite board, with the help of a support boat. Three months later Anne Quemere achieved an unassisted crossing on an 18-foot (5.5-m) kite boat. Meanwhile, far from being put off from ever going to sea again after his close brush with death, Dom was back two years later with another plan: to break the thirty-five-day record for rowing across the Atlantic. He and his team missed the record by just two days.

Eleven months later *Little Murka* turned up off the coast of Ireland, only a few barnacles the worse for her 2,500-mile (4,000-km) journey.

movistar

Overall length
70 ft. (21 m)

Waterline length
64 ft. (19.5 m)

Draft
15 ft. (4.6 m)

Beam
20 ft. (6 m)

Displacement
49 tons

Sail area
7,600 sq. ft. (706 m²)

Interesting facts
The Volvo Ocean Race started life in 1973 as the Whitbread Race, a round-the-world competition in four legs, starting and finishing in Portsmouth. Seventeen yachts took part, racing on handicap; three sailors were lost at sea.

The race was run every four years until 2001 when sponsorship was taken over by Volvo and it became known as the Volvo Ocean Race.

In 1993 the Whitbread 60 class was designed specifically for the race and from 1997 was the only type of boat that was allowed to compete in the race. In 2005 it was replaced by the Volvo Open 70—a high-speed, lightweight skimming dish of a boat, more akin to the nervy Open 60s, and very susceptible to damage. There have been changes made for the 2008-9 race, including a maximum weight for keel, fin and bulb of 7.4 tons, a reduction in overall weight range of the boat to 13.8–14 tons (previously 12.5–14 tons), a ban on bomb doors to prevent water entry, and a ban on titanium in keel rams to reduce costs and increase reliability of the boats.

The signs were all there. Despite recurring problems with her keel,
movistar carried on sailing in the 2005–06 Volvo Ocean Race,
even at one point reaching an impressive third place. Then, while
crossing the Atlantic and only 300 miles from land, she began to sink.
And this time it was serious.

That Sinking Feeling

Bouwe Bekking (2006)

We are sinking! Everybody up! Slow the boat down—the water is coming in very fast—and close the water tight hatches." These words greeted the crew of *movistar*, the Spanish entry in the 2005–06 Volvo Ocean Race, in the early hours of March 2, 2006—not what you want to hear from your skipper as you are approaching Cape Horn in the middle of a round-the-world yacht race. *movistar* was on the fourth leg of the race from New Zealand to Rio de Janeiro, when the keel box containing the keel mechanism started to leak. By the time the alarm was raised, both the generator and the engine were underwater and fuses were popping all over the place, disabling those all-important bilge pumps. Meanwhile, the cabin was awash with sails, sleeping bags, food, and other debris, creating a scene that Dutch skipper Bouwe Bekking likened to something "Hitchcock could only dream of."

"A sailor's nightmare is sinking," he reported to race headquarters, "and this looks like a pretty serious situation. If we had rats on board, they would have jumped off by now."

Thanks to the quick thinking of crew member Chris Nicholson, who dove underwater to connect the emergency bilge pumps directly to the batteries, the boat was slowly pumped out, and a few hours later the crew was able to make an emergency repair. Two

days later the yacht pulled into Ushuaia in southern Argentina to make a more permanent fix and to allow them to finish the leg.

It wasn't the first time *movistar* had had problems with her keel, and it wouldn't be the last. On the first night of the race, the Spanish boat and the American boat, *Pirates of the Caribbean*, had suffered keel damage and had to pull into harbor to make repairs. Both boats were eventually shipped to Cape Town for the second leg rather than sailing there on their own bottoms. Halfway through the second leg, *movistar* had more keel trouble and had to pull in at Albany, Western Australia, for repairs. Two days later the ram broke again, which meant they were unable to cant, or angle, it to the optimum position. Two other boats also had problems with their keels on that leg, and one of them, *Ericsson*, had to be shipped to Australia. It was a bad start for the new Volvo Open 70 class on their first serious test, and questions were soon being asked about the integrity of the boats.

It was all a long way from the launch of the event in 1973, then known as the Whitbread Round the World Race, and a mismatched collection of seventeen yachts raced the seven legs of the race on handicap. In an attempt to level the playing field, the Whitbread 60 class was introduced in 1993, ruling out the popular cruising class and putting the whole

Seven boats from six different countries took part in the 2005–06 Volvo Ocean Race, each with a crew of ten (twelve are allowed if it's an all-woman crew). Five sailors have died in the race during its thirty-two-year history.

event on a more professional footing. By 2005, however, these boats had been outdated and were replaced by the Volvo Open 70, which were 10 feet (3 m) longer than their predecessors and with the wide, shallow hulls typical of most modern ocean racers. Seven teams lined up for the 2005–06 race, which now comprised nine legs plus a new element of match racing during seven of the stopovers.

Once the team had completed the keel repairs in Rio de Janeiro, *movistar* carried gamely up the Atlantic, coming in second on the fifth leg to Baltimore and winning the in-port races there. On May 18, as she was crossing the Atlantic Ocean from New York to Portsmouth, England, the boat was enjoying ideal sailing conditions, surfing down the waves at 24 knots. This was the kind of sailing for which the crew had signed up. Then they received news of a man overboard on a rival boat. Spinnaker trimmer Hans Horrevoets had been swept over the side of *ABN AMRO TWO* just minutes before going down below to put on his harness. The Dutch entry had performed a textbook rescue but were unable to resuscitate their man. The Atlantic had claimed its first victim of the race.

Two days later *movistar* had her own problems. Sailing off a wind of 22 to 27 knots, with big following seas and a triple-reefed mainsail to reduce sail area exposed to the wind, the crew heard a loud crack. Rushing below, Bekking first checked the rams, which looked fine, and then the keel pin. To his horror he discovered that the aft end of the pin, on which the entire 9,920-lb. (4,500-kg) keel pivoted, had shifted by 2 inches (50 mm). Water was pouring in, and it was only a matter of time before the whole thing dropped off.

Bekking immediately alerted race control, and the other Volvo boats in the area were put on alert for a possible rescue. Ironically, *ABN AMRO TWO*, whose crew was still coming to terms with their own bereavement, was nearest and was asked to turn back to go to the assistance of the stricken yacht.

Meanwhile, the *movistar* crew, desperate to stay in the race, were carrying out their own emergency repairs. Following the advice of a structural engineer, relayed via radio by its shore team, the crew drilled a hole through the deck. They then attached a Spectra fastening from the boom fitting on the mast through the hole to the keel itself to prevent it from dropping any farther. Two halyard lines, used for raising or lowering sails, were also fed through from the mast and attached to the pin in an attempt to hoist it back in place. This seemed to do the trick, and the bilge pump was able to cope with the amount of water coming in. At 1:00 A.M. the following day, Bekking reported that the situation was stable and that they would be able to bring the boat into port on their own, "fingers crossed."

A few hours later, however, the situation had deteriorated. "This morning we shifted over on the other board to check how the keel would cope with that angle," he told race control. "Straightaway we saw that the water intake nearly doubled and we had to start the second emergency pump. That made me realize that we were actually in bigger trouble."

Approximately 307 miles (495 km) from Land's End—the most westerly point in England—and with winds of 50 knots forecasted, Bekking made the call to abandon ship. It was, he said, "the hardest decision I [have] ever taken in my life." *ABN AMRO TWO*, which was still on standby, was asked to rescue the ten people on board *movistar*. With *ABN AMRO TWO* hovering nearby, one of the two life rafts was then

"Ten lives at stake, with a similar number of families, [I made] the right call... There is no mirror on board here, but I could face myself, we have done everything possible."

launched, and the crew floated over to their new home, taking enough food with them to last until they arrived in the United Kingdom. The second life raft was transferred over to *ABN AMRO TWO* uninflated, just in case the worst should happen again. Bekking had one last look down below, and that was it. End of race, end of boat. There was nothing more he could do. "Ten lives at stake, with a similar number of families, [I made] the right call," he wrote soon after from *ABN AMRO TWO*. "There is no mirror on board here, but I could face myself, we have done everything possible."

Meanwhile, the Royal Navy had responded to the call for help by sending the fishery patrol vessel HMS *Mersey* "with all possible speed" from Milford Haven to escort the crews back to safety.

Back on board *ABN AMRO TWO*, the *movistar* crew was reduced to observer status, because the Dutch team wanted to carry on racing in memory of their crewmate. It was a symbolic gesture suggested by Hans's father, who believed that his son would have wanted the crew to proceed. On May 23, off the Cornish coast near Falmouth, the body of Hans Horrevoets was transferred to the Dutch frigate HNLMS *Van Galen* to be taken back to Terheijden, his hometown in the Netherlands. A minute of silence was held on board *ABN AMRO TWO* before they continued racing to Portsmouth. They arrived long after the other boats but received an emotional welcome.

For the crew of *movistar*, however, the race wasn't over yet. They still hoped to salvage the yacht that, despite her tendency to break and try her best to sink, had nevertheless carried them into third place overall at the point of abandonment. Before leaving her, they had set sea anchors from the stern so that she would continue to sail. The generators were also left running and her satellite communication systems left on so she could be tracked more easily. The following day, however, the signal disappeared, and when the *movistar* shore team flew over the area three days later, there was no sign of her. It was time to move on.

Indian

Bambola Quatre
TRANSVenture
Suez TFI

Bambola Quatre

Overall length
36 ft. (11 m)

Waterline length
30 ft. (9 m)

Beam
12 ft. 4 in. (3.7 m)

Draft
5 ft. (1.5 m)

Designer
Angus Primrose

Make
Moody 36

Interesting facts
It is estimated that, since 1996, some 200 yachts have been victims of pirate attacks and that around twenty yachts have gone missing. Historically, the most dangerous areas are the Sulu Sea in the Philippines, the Malacca Strait, between Malaysia and Sumatra, and the Gulf of Aden, between Yemen and Somalia. The north coast of South America is another, relatively recent hot spot. The worse year for piracy was 2000, when 471 ships (mainly commercial) were attacked worldwide.

Opinions about whether or not to carry a gun on a cruising yacht vary, with some arguing that it is an essential means of self-defense, while others suggest that producing a gun is only going to escalate the situation and that a pirate will invariably come off better in a shoot-out. Michael Briant states that he wouldn't carry a gun.

Suggestions for avoiding pirate attacks include considering sailing without navigational lights in order to be harder to spot, or asking for an escort from coalition forces.

A former director of the popular British television series *Howards' Way* thought he'd been through it all: storms, shipwrecks, and even being hit by lightning. But then Michael Briant found himself in the Gulf of Aden with a gun in his stomach. It was just like something out of the movies.

Pirates!

Michael Briant (2003)

They appeared through the early morning haze: Three lifeboats from an old ship were heading toward *Bambola Quatre* on the starboard bow. *Bambola* was sailing 30 miles (48 km) off the coast of Yemen, heading up the Gulf of Aden toward the East African country of Djibouti at the end of a three-year circumnavigation. Owner Michael Briant was on watch in the cockpit of the 36-foot (11-m) yacht, while his wife, Monique, was asleep in the rear cabin and their 21-year-old crew member Alex slept in the forward cabin. Behind them was another yacht, the 35-foot (10-m) *Josephine*, whose owner, the German single-hander Ulf Reimer, was sleeping while his boat navigated on autopilot. Briant was keeping watch for both yachts.

As the lifeboats approached, Briant could see that their sides were raised with blue plastic sheeting to keep the waves out of their overloaded hulls. They were packed with people.

"My first thought was that they were 'boat people' lost and in need of food or water," he said. "My second thought was that with that many, we didn't have enough to make a difference. My third thought was, it was perhaps a problem."

Briant rushed below and radioed the skipper of *Josephine* to warn him that they had visitors. As Briant spoke on the radio, he heard gunshots outside. While looking out of the hatch, he saw some of the men on the lifeboats firing machine guns in the air and shouting for him to stop. It looked as if these people were after more than just food and water. He went back down below, switched the radio over to the emergency channel, and sent out a Mayday, giving the yacht's position and explaining that they were under attack by pirates. A reply came almost immediately.

"This is a U.S. Navy warship. Repeat your position."

"We are 13° 31' north, 48° 24' east," Briant said. "And they are shooting!"

"We are 20 miles (32 km) to the north, heading toward you," came the reply.

He heard more shots being fired outside and climbed back into the cockpit. One of the boats was now just a few yards away, and several of the men were pointing their guns straight at him. He feared for his life, but more than that, he feared for his wife, Monique, and prayed that she would stay down below deck; otherwise, things could get really nasty.

The former child star turned director had started sailing in his late twenties, when Monique gave him a *Mirror* dinghy kit to build. He was immediately hooked and joined the BBC's sailing club on the River Thames, although racing success

somehow always eluded him. At this point he was directing several successful British television shows. As his career developed, his boats gradually increased in size and his cruising range extended, eventually including the Mediterranean Sea and the Canary Islands. Work and pleasure finally came together when he directed the BBC series *Howards' Way*. Because its soap-opera plot revolved around a hypothetical boatyard somewhere on the south coast of England, it was the perfect subject matter for this man of the sea.

> They had experienced bad weather, witnessed shipwrecks, and even been struck by lightning, but this was the first time they had been attacked by pirates.

Following the success of *Howards' Way*, Briant moved to Holland and had a lucrative career in television. But he never lost his love of sailing. Monique was a bit less enthusiastic but went along with her husband's hobby. In 2000 the couple bought a Moody 36, a popular and spacious modern cruiser, and set off around the world. The trip took them to Greece, Turkey, Trinidad, Panama, the

South Pacific, Australia, New Zealand, and Indonesia. They had experienced bad weather, witnessed shipwrecks, and were even struck by lightning, but this was the first time they had been attacked by pirates.

By now the men on the lifeboats were getting angry and demanding that Briant lower his sails. Alex, now on deck, pulled down the mainsail while Briant furled the genoa. With a crunch two of the pirate boats came alongside *Bambola*, and several gunmen came on board. Briant noticed that the rest of the people on the lifeboats—men, women, and children of all ages—looked terrified as well. He concluded that they were probably refugees from Somalia smuggled over the Yemen border and were victims as well.

One of the gunmen went down below and immediately headed toward the aft cabin, where Monique was sleeping. Briant held his breath. But in a moment the man was back, demanding that Briant go below. Once in the saloon, one of the yacht's communal areas, he shoved his gun in Briant's ribs, rubbed his thumb and index fingers together in front of his face, and shouted, "Money, money! Dollar, dollar!"

"Okay," Briant replied calmly, and went into the rear cabin to find the cash. He noted that the duvet was piled up on the bed and assumed that Monique was hiding underneath.

Back in the saloon, he handed over $600 in cash. As the man started counting, another gunman came down below. A quarrel erupted, and the two men started fighting over the money. As Briant backed away, he was called on deck by another of the attackers. The pirate demanded the ship's binoculars and Briant's watch and then took Alex's expensive diving watch as well. Neither of *Bambola's* crew

Bambola moored in La Rochelle on the west coast of France during one of Briant's many sailing trips abroad.

Briant and his wife enjoyed sailing all over the world before being attacked by pirates in the Gulf of Aden.

In order to reach the Suez Canal, yachts must pass through the Red Sea via the Gulf of Aden, where they become easy targets for pirates.

resisted, knowing that the consequence could be a bullet through the gut.

After resolving their quarrel, the two men emerged from the saloon, clutching the yacht's two

As the lifeboats crunched alongside again, the men passed over the stolen equipment and climbed back onto a lifeboat. The next minute they were gone, heading off to the northeast, toward Yemen.

radio transmitters and whatever pieces of electronic equipment they managed to disconnect. Still pointing their guns at Briant and Alex, they shouted

at their colleagues to row back and get them. As the lifeboats crunched alongside again, the men passed over the stolen equipment and climbed back onto a lifeboat. The next minute they were gone, heading off to the northeast, toward Yemen.

Still shaking, Briant hurried down below to look for Monique. He pulled the duvet off the bed, but there was no sign of his wife. Where could she be? Then he noticed that the bathroom door was closed. He opened it, and to his relief, found her inside—fully dressed and smoking a cigarette. Ever the reluctant

sailor, Monique looked none too pleased at this latest turn of events, and Briant knew he would have some explaining to do.

By this time, the other yacht was on her way over. It turned out that Reimer had a lucky escape. When the third lifeboat started firing at his mast and demanding him to stop, he pretended not to understand. He then went below, loaded his flare gun and shot it out of the hatch. The shot was enough for the two gunmen, who then decided to focus their attention on *Bambola* instead.

Five minutes later the U.S. naval vessel arrived and, after checking that the crew of both yachts were unharmed, left in pursuit of the pirates. For a while Briant felt hopeful that he might actually get some of his money and equipment back. They later heard that, although the ship had caught up with the lifeboats, for some reason, no one had been arrested. Despite being in international waters, the American navy was reluctant to police the seaways in the way Briant had hoped they might.

It turned out that *Bambola*'s crew was lucky. That year, the authorities reported the worst figures ever for piracy; there were 234 attacks, sixteen deaths, and fifty-two people injured around the world. It could have been much worse. But that was small comfort for Briant. "Only one percent of the yachts heading for the Red Sea are actually boarded and robbed in any one season," he acknowledged. "I just hated being that statistic."

Although "policed" by U.S. warships, most of the Gulf of Aden is in international waters and therefore not under their jurisdiction.

TRANSVenture

Overall length
23 ft. (7 m)

Beam
7 ft. (2 m)

Depth of hull
7 ft. (2 m)

Weight fully laden
1 ton

Interesting facts
By 2001 only one person had succeeded in rowing across the Indian ocean: the 43-year-old Anders Svedlund. The Swedish-born naturalized New Zealander set off from Kalbarri in Australia on April 21, 1971, and arrived in Madagascar sixty-four days later. His record would remain unbroken for three decades.

On his first attempt in 1970, Svedlund capsized after three days at sea and had to row back to Australia.

Ocean rowing is a challenge that many teams undertake to raise money for charity. In 2006 Stu Turnbull and Ed Bayliss of the United Kingdom rowed across the Atlantic from the Canary Islands to Antigua to raise money for Cancer Research UK. In 2007 Dom Mee and his team attempted to row across the Atlantic from the Canary Islands to Barbados in under thirty-five days to raise money for the children's charity Barnados. Unfortunately, they missed out on the record by two days.

Teamwork and comraderie were at the heart of Rob Abernethy and Mike Noel-Smith's bid to break the Indian Ocean rowing record. But tragedy struck when, after surviving storms and bad jokes, one of the former army officers received a life-threatening injury.

There Is no I in Team

Mike Noel-Smith and Rob Abernethy (2003)

The plan was straightforward enough: to row across the Indian Ocean from Australia to La Réunion and, on the way, raise money for charity. There were several records up for grabs: fastest crossing, if they could beat the sixty-four-day time set by Anders Svedlund in 1971; the first two-man row; and the first British rowers to complete the voyage. Rob Abernethy and Mike Noel-Smith were well suited for the challenge: Both served in the army—Rob in the Far East and Mike in Northern Ireland. Both men played rugby and now spent time running leadership courses. Neither of them had any rowing experience, but a six-month training program run by the British Olympic Medical Center provided some background.

It was 3,750 miles (6,000 km) from their starting point of Carnarvon in Western Australia to the island of La Réunion, which meant they would have to average nearly 60 miles (96 km) a day to beat the record. To achieve this, they planned to row continuously taking turns, two hours on and two hours off, whenever the weather allowed. Their vessel was the 23-foot (7-m) *TRANSVenture*, which was fitted with state-of-the-art navigation and communication equipment and enough food to last them eighty days—just in case. If successful, they hoped to raise $450,000 (£250,000) for Sparks, a children's medical research charity.

The stakes had risen dramatically a few weeks before their departure by the news that their fellow Brit, Simon Chalk, had just left on the same journey from nearby Kalbari. They would have to have exceptional good luck if they were to catch up with him now.

Taking advantage of a good weather window, they set off just before midnight on April 19, 2003, and quickly got into their stride, clocking more than 50 miles (80 km) in their first twenty-four hours. By the third day it was so hot that they were able to cook their "boil-in-the-bag" food on deck without using the stove. Wildlife was plentiful, and they were soon spotting flying fish, tuna, puffinlike birds, and their first shark, a 7-foot (2-m)-long specimen that circled the boat a couple of times before heading off to find more palatable prey.

By the sixth day, however, the weather had deteriorated and, with 20-knot winds and 25-foot (7.6-m) swells lashing the boat, they were forced to set the para-anchor (a development of the sea anchor) and take shelter in the boat's small cabin—more of a survival capsule than a real cabin. "It looks like a wall of water approaching the boat, and when we are on the crest of a wave, you can literally look down into a valley of water down to the trough," reported Mike. "It is too dangerous to be out on deck." It was

With no rowing experience before they set off, Rob (pictured) and Mike went through a rigorous Olympic training program to get them up to speed.

their first experience spending any length of time in the cabin, and the consensus was that it was "cramped and hot," though the BBC World Service brought some relief.

Two days later they were rowing again, and in their second week they clocked a nonstop seventy-hour stint before another storm forced them back into their "sweatbox." At the same time, their water maker, which they relied on for all their fresh water, broke down and, despite repeated attempts to fix it, refused to cooperate again. Their only alternative, apart from collecting rainwater, was a hand-operated water maker, which required 1,000 pumps to produce a single bucket of water. From now on, whenever they weren't rowing, they would spend half of their "off" time working the pump to produce the water essential for their survival. Worse still, for a pair of self-confessed caffeine addicts, they were forced to give up tea and coffee because of the dehydration risk.

By May 11 they were back in their cabin, this time amusing themselves by drawing up their ultimate teams for a fantasy British Lions versus the Rest of the World rugby match. Living at such close quarters twenty-four hours a day would be a test for the best relationship, but Rob and Mike overcame their differences through a classic survival technique: humor. As a result, morale remained high throughout the voyage—a fact that was to prove very important to them both. "We motivate each other by not

wanting to let each other down; as a consequence, we work really well together," wrote Mike. "We both have our reasons for doing this row. Some are the same and some different, but we are both totally focused on crossing the ocean as quickly as we can. To do that when times are tough requires a great deal of motivation and teamwork. It's great to be putting into practice what we teach back home in an environment that could hardly be more extreme. It gives us faith that what we teach in our 'day jobs' is correct."

By May 30, after forty-two days at sea, the pair seemed to be in their element. Strong following winds were driving them along, and *TRANSVenture* was surfing down the waves at speeds of up to 10 knots. Their daily tally was up to 85 miles (137 km), and they were approaching the halfway mark—still a long way off the record, but at last making up for the time lost early in the journey.

As conditions worsened, however, Mike was thrown out of his seat, causing him to smash his head against the side of the boat. Knocked unconscious, only the harness he was wearing stopped him from being thrown overboard into the foaming sea. Although Rob initially described his teammate as just "a bit groggy," he soon realized that the situation was more serious. "I am pretty sure Mike is suffering from concussion," he told his shore team the following day. "As we have both have had concussion during our rugby careers, we

recognize the symptoms, and Mike has them."
By now the wind was up to 35 knots, and the pair
were being thrown about in their cabin "like rag
dolls." Their water supply was running out, too,
and with the storm raging outside, they were unable
to use the water pump to make more.

That night, the para-anchor broke loose, and
Rob was forced to set the reserve sea anchor, which
was unable to cope with the severity of the storm,
causing the boat to drift sideways on to the waves.
It was only a matter of
time before the boat
capsized, and on the
third night of the storm,
the boat rolled over and
remained inverted for
several anxious minutes

"Over the past seventy-two hours we have suffered physical damage to our bodies and structural damage to the boat to the extent that it is unwise and reckless to continue."

before righting herself. Meanwhile, the structure
of the boat started to disintegrate—the rudder was
already destroyed, and the panels of the aft cabin
were starting to creak alarmingly. Soon the reserve
sea anchor also sheered away, and *TRANSVenture*
was left to skid across the waves.

As Mike lapsed in and out of consciousness, the
team issued a Mayday with a request for immediate
assistance from the Australian Rescue services.
"Over the past seventy-two hours we have suffered
physical damage to our bodies and structural damage
to the boat to the extent that it is unwise and reckless
to continue," Rob explained. "Mike's head is in a bad

way. He has also broken his nose and damaged his
eye and needs medical attention ASAP to ensure that
there are no serious complications."

Closest to the scene was the Australian frigate
HMAS *Newcastle*, which was immediately dispatched
to their aid. It was the end of the adventure for
Mike, although there was speculation that Rob might
continue alone. He soon put aside that idea, however,
saying: "Mike and I started this together, and although
I would love to crack on and finish this for everyone,
not only is the boat unable to do so, I feel that my
place is with my mate as he returns to shore.
There is no I in team."

The two men and their boat were rescued by
Newcastle on June 4, and Mike made a full recovery
from his injuries. Once home, they continued to
teach the lessons of leadership and teamwork.
Ten days after their rescue, their rival, Simon
Chalk, arrived in Mauritius to become the first
British person to row across the Indian Ocean—
although his time of 108 days was well outside the
overall record.

After forty-four
days at sea, with the
boat damaged by
storms and Mike
suffering from a
concussion, the
two men are rescued
by an Australian
navy warship.

Suez TFI

Overall length
26 ft. (7.8 m)

Beam
4 ft. (1.3 m)

Draft
3 ft. (1.05 m)

Weight
1,100–1,200 lb. (500–550 kg)

Sail area
56–80 sq. ft. (5.2–7.4 m²)

Designed
Guy Saillard

Built
Estuaire Plaisance Services

Interesting facts
Born in May 1960, Raphaëla qualified as a veterinary surgeon and lives in Brittany, northwest France. In April 2000, she became the first woman to cross the Atlantic on a sail board, sailing from Saly in Senegal to the island of Martinique in fifty-six days.

In the summer of 2002, she became the first person to cross the Mediterranean Sea on a sail board, sailing 550 miles (885 km) from Marseille in the South of France to Sidi Bou Saïd in Tunisia in ten days.

In November 2003, she became the first person to cross the Pacific Ocean on a sail board, traveling 4,455 miles (7,170 km) from Lima in Peru to Tahiti in eighty-nine days. Her latest adventure was to windsurf around the coast of Brittany from St. Malo to La Baule.

As well as highlighting environmental issues, Raphaëla campaigns to promote better education services in developing countries through her chosen charity, Aide et Action.

She'd already crossed the Atlantic and the Pacific on a sail board, so the Indian Ocean should have been...well, plain sailing. But then Raphaëla le Gouvello was struck by the dreaded mal de mer...

A Fishy Menu

Raphaëla le Gouvello (2006)

The Indian Ocean is the third largest body of water in the world. Some 3,262 nautical miles (6,041 km) separate Northwest Australia from the French island of La Réunion, off the Madagascar coast. Its average depth is 12,760 feet (3,890 m), and it covers approximately 20 percent of the Earth's water surface. The United States would fit inside the area of this vast sea mass seven and a half times.

Despite this almost unimaginable size, for the lone sailor navigating the Indian Ocean aboard a small boat, life can seem very restricted and small. Claustrophobically small for some. Take Raphaëla le Gouvello, the French sailor who attempted to cross this mighty ocean on a sail board, unsupported and completely alone. At 26 feet (7.8 m) long and 4 feet (1.3 m) wide, her board was relatively large, but once the vessel's overhangs were taken into account, she was left with just 22 feet (6.8 m) by 4 feet (1.14 m) of deck space. Beneath that, squeezed into a space of little more than 35 cubic feet (1 m³), was a small cabin—just long enough for her to lie in—and keep enough equipment and supplies to sustain her for two months.

Despite her constricted living conditions, le Gouvello was well equipped for the journey. In addition to Very High Frequency radio and Global Positioning Systems, the board was equipped with two Iridium phones (one fixed and one mobile), a

laptop computer, and a watermaker, all powered by four 120-amp batteries, which were charged by eight solar panels fitted to the side of the hull. Along with tools and various spares, she carried lights, distress flares, a stove and spare gas cartridges, a first-aid kit, a survival suit and survival blankets, books, and an MP3 player. For sustenance she had freeze-dried meals, dried meat, dried fruit, energy bars, crackers, and condensed milk—making up a total of 220 lb. (100 kg) of food. Fully loaded, the board weighed over 1100 lb. (500 kg).

But while some of her equipment may have been high tech, her means of propulsion was as old as the sea itself: the wind. Le Gouvello's sail board set a single sail fitted with a "wishbone" boom and carbon fiber mast, and she carried four sails, ranging in size from 56 to 80 square feet (5.2 to 7.4 m²), to match the varying weather conditions. It took her up to an hour every morning to choose the right size sail for that day's weather and rig it to the mast and boom. Changing the sail once she was under way was not a good option.

After waiting a week for cyclones to pass, le Gouvello finally departed from Exmouth in Western Australia on April 9, 2006. Her objective: to be the first solo windsurfer to cross the Indian Ocean. After suffering from seasickness during previous crossings of the Atlantic and the Pacific, she took the precaution of wearing an anti-seasickness patch for the first day or so. The result, it seemed, was merely to postpone the illness because, by the second day, thirst and headaches began. Her appetite, however, was fine. "I eat 80 percent of my daily food ration, which is not too bad," she told her support team back in France in one of her twice-daily phone updates. "All the same, the food I've got is not so good, and I always take out the same stuff: Moroccan lamb or sweet chicken."

Meals followed a carefully calculated pattern aimed at providing le Gouvello with a daily intake of 3,300 calories. Breakfast, at around 7:00 A.M., was composed of freeze-dried granola rehydrated with warm water, followed by bread and jam and a flask of tea. Lunch, at around 1:00 P.M., was a rehydrated freeze-dried main dish, such as pasta with meat sauce, followed by dried fruit or cookies for dessert. Dinner was another rehydrated meal, such as paella, followed again by dried fruit or cookies. "Eating, especially the evening meal, becomes a special time," she wrote.

"For at sea, like in space, for a person traveling alone, mealtimes constitute a tenuous and emotional link with life on Earth. I still feel as though I'm 'cooking' when I choose my lunch and dinner meals. I vary the spices, adding a sprig of tarragon here, a few basil leaves there, a lot of olive oil, more and more red pepper, curry, and soy sauce. I mix everything together, placing an evergrowing emphasis on the seasonings." Food that appealed to her in a supermarket in Fremantle, Australia, however, might repulse her once she was at sea. Likewise, something that may have been a favorite while she was sailing in the Pacific might no longer appeal in the Indian Ocean. "Your body adapts and tells you what it needs. You have to learn to listen to it. As time goes on, the cravings change, you get tired or literally sick of one food or another, and you can't control it. Sometimes you can actually gag at the thought of a certain food." Among other delights packed by her overenthusiastic shore crew in Australia included crocodile jerky (dried crocodile meat), kangaroo, and emu. And at first

Le Gouvello's living space was cramped, to say the least: 35 cubic feet (1 m³) in which to cook, sleep, navigate, communicate, and perform all personal functions.

the jerky seemed to hit the spot. "That wasn't bad at all," le Gouvello reported. "Tasted different."

By the second week, however, her seasickness seemed to be getting worse. Unable to keep any food down, she was even finding the water unpalatable. To avoid carrying large tanks of water, the board was fitted with a desalination machine that could convert salt water to fresh at the rate of 1.3 gallons (5 L) per hour—although the water often had a strange taste. Concerned that she might become ill, her doctor asked her to mix a bit of salt in her drinking water, but le Gouvello couldn't find her box of salt and felt too queasy for a lengthy search.

On April 18 she received the news that she had long suspected: She wasn't just seasick; she was almost certainly suffering from gastroenteritis. It would take about ten days to recover. Although her condition wasn't yet life threatening, she knew that it could be if she went ten days without food. Therefore, despite her constant queasiness, she would have to make herself eat. "I'm forcing myself to ingest three grains of rice and to drink a mouthful of water with a little jam," she told her shore crew. "Right now I dream of being hungry and wolfing down a whole dish of pasta."

Despite being weakened by what she described as "a race against nausea," le Gouvello kept up her routine: sailing for six to seven hours a day in 1-to 2-hour stints, with 15-minute breaks in between each stint. At night she stowed the sail, rigged a half-size mast in the centerboard slot with a flashlight and set her small "drift sail." In case of a capsize, a large orange float was attached to the aft deck, which was buoyant enough to right the board again should it go over. Unlike most single-handed sailors on large yachts, who sleep in 20-minute naps, le Gouvello was allowed a luxurious six to seven hours' sleep at night before getting up and starting her routine again.

When the weather was too rough to sail—or, indeed, if there was no wind at all—le Gouvello set her sea anchor and settled in her bunk to read a book or listen to her MP3 player. *The Constant Gardener* by John le Carré, *One Hundred Years of Solitude* by Gabriel García Márquez, *Doggy Bag* by Philippe Djian, and a book about the Réunion Islands were among her Indian Ocean selection. Dvorak's New World Symphony was also a constant musical favorite.

Le Gouvello endured two weeks of misery, struggling to overcome nausea as the board rolled

constantly in the Indian Ocean swell. But by April 27 she had recovered her appetite enough to tackle the oatmeal. "It's delicious, quite nutritive, not too sweet; when hot, it's really perfect. And I have also found the apple pie—quite good, too, provided you don't eat the horrible pastry." Back in France her shore crew breathed a sigh of relief. Le Gouvello was back in form.

The rest of her crossing was not without incident—stormy weather was followed by calm, the board capsized, a sail tried to escape over the side, and the board capsized again, but at least she had her health back. With a healthy body she could deal with whatever the Indian Ocean threw at her. Day by day she counted the distance down, collecting goose barnacles to be analyzed by one of her colleagues back home, washing her clothes, and keeping the board in good shape. For nearly two months she stayed within the confines of her board—stepping outside only when she had to scrub its bottom or when she was swept off by a wave.

When le Gouvello arrived in Réunion on June 8, 2006, she had been sailing for 60 days, 2 hours, and 1 minute. No wonder she told reporters that she wouldn't be tackling any oceans ever again. Yet barely a year later, she was off once more, this time to sail 400 miles (645 km) around the Brittany coast. But at least this time she was unlikely to find any crocodile jerky hidden in her food supply.

Le Gouvello arriving in La Réunion. The plucky 44-year-old suffered debilitating seasickness and was unable to eat for much of her sixty days at sea.

Southern

Endurance / James Caird

Endurance
Overall length
144 ft. (43.9 m)

Beam
25 ft. (7.6 m)

Displacement
350 tons

Built
Framnæs shipyards,
Sandefjord, Norway

Launched
1912

James Caird
Overall length
23 ft. (7 m)

Beam
6 ft. 9 in. (2 m)

Draft
2 ft. 6 in. (76 cm)

Interesting facts
A few weeks after *Endurance* set sail for the Weddell Sea, another ship, *Aurora*, left for McMurdo Sound on the other side of Antarctica. Its task was to lay a trail of supplies for Shackleton and his men to pick up on the final phase of their crossing.

While the depots were being built, however, a storm blew *Aurora* out to sea, leaving ten men stranded on shore. They continued with their task, convinced that the main expedition was on its way and would be depending on their supplies. By the time Shackleton appeared in *Aurora* to rescue them, three men had died and all but four dogs had been killed. The crew had been on the ice for almost two years.

After the *Endurance* sank beneath the Antarctic ice, her crew of twenty-eight men were left stranded in one of the most inhospitable places on earth. Their only hope of rescue lay across 800 miles (1,300 km) of the Southern Ocean, and the only boat they had to make the journey was a 23-foot (7-m) open whaler. It was Sir Ernest Shackleton's last bid for glory.

The Last Prize

Ernest Shackleton (1914)

Look at the southernmost tip of South America and the northernmost tip of Antarctica and you'll see they are both skewed to one side. It's as if someone punched a massive hole between them and the land is still torn and shedding into the ocean. And, in some ways, that's exactly what happened. In between these two continents runs the mighty Southern Ocean, fighting its way relentlessly around the world like a punch-drunk boxer. This stretch of water, with the dreaded Cape Horn on one side and the ice floes of the Antarctic on the other, has given rise to the old sailor's adage: "Below 40 degrees, there is no law, but below 50 degrees, there is no God."

It's not a place to venture out in on a boat, much less a 23-foot (7-m) wooden ship's tender. Yet that is exactly what Sir Ernest Shackleton proposed doing during the winter of 1916. As he set out from Elephant Island, on the tip of Antarctica, he and his crew of five had only rudimentary equipment and had none of the standard safety devices that sailors carry today—not even a radio. A makeshift canvas deck kept the water out of the boat, and boulders picked up off the beach were their only form of ballast. If their frail craft—no more than an overgrown dinghy—capsized, they would certainly die. The lives of twenty-two men, left behind on the island, depended on them reaching the island of South Georgia, 800 miles

(1,300 km) to the north. And the only way to get to South Georgia was across the Southern Ocean.

The journey had started almost two years before, when the expedition set off from Plymouth, United Kingdom, in August 1914 on the 350-ton *Endurance* bound for Antarctica. It was three years after Roald Amundsen had beaten Captain Robert Scott to the South Pole, and Shackleton was determined to restore British national pride by going one further than the Norwegian. His plan was to be the first to cross from one side of the continent to the other—a feat that had been attempted only once before, unsuccessfully. As *Endurance* navigated through the Weddell Sea, however, she became trapped by pack ice and her crew of twenty-eight men and sixty-nine dogs spent nine months waiting for the ice to release them from its clutches. But as spring arrived, instead of melting, the ice floes moved in closer, slowly crushing the vessel to death. As the ship's massive oak frames broke with "pistol-like cracks," the men tried desperately to stem the flow of water, but the ice was inexorable. On October 27 the *Endurance* succumbed to the inevitable, and four weeks later she finally sank beneath the ice.

With his main base now lost, Shackleton was forced to give up the expedition, and he turned his attention to getting everyone home safely. After

Twenty-two men were left behind on Elephant Island and survived for four months on leftover rations and seal meat. They made shelters by turning their boats upside down over simple stone walls.

several attempts to cross overland to the whaling station at Paulet Island, he and his men gave up and decided to use the three small ship's boats they had rescued from the *Endurance* to sail to Deception Island, 200 miles (320 km) to the west. They knew that provisions were stored there for shipwrecked mariners, and they also hoped that they might meet up with a passing whaling ship. By then, seal and penguin meat was their main diet. They tried to conserve their dwindling supplies of packaged rations, and even the dogs had all been killed and eaten.

After a few days at sea in temperatures as low as -22°F (-30°C), some of the men were already suffering

from frostbite, and they pulled in at Elephant Island—one of the fragments of land torn from the tip of the Antarctic Peninsula. It was a barren, inhospitable place, buffeted continually by Southern Ocean gales. After sixteen months in the Antarctic, Shackleton and his men were reaching the limit of their endurance. Yet they were now hundreds of miles away from the shipping routes, with only enough rations for five weeks—or three months, if supplemented with seal and penguin meat. Their prospects looked bleak.

As Shackleton stared across the angry sea—turned white by spray and snow—he knew that their only hope of survival was for some of them to cross to the

Born in Ireland in 1874, Shackleton had already been on two Arctic expeditions: once with Scott in 1901 and again, with his own team, in 1907.

other side and organize a rescue party to come back for the rest. Almost directly north lay the Falkland Islands, 500 miles (800 km) away, but they would have to sail against the prevailing northwesterly winds to reach them. Farther east, and therefore downwind of them, lay South Georgia, 800 miles (1,300 km) away across the roughest ocean in the world. It seemed to be a mad undertaking in the small boats they had at their disposal, but it was their only chance.

Shackleton chose the lightest but most seaworthy of the three boats, the 23-foot (7-m)-long whaler *James Caird*, and had the ship's carpenter rig a canvas deck over most of it to keep the worst weather out.

He picked five men to accompany him and took enough provisions to last them four weeks—if they didn't make it to South Georgia in that time, they would probably be dead anyway. Their only instruments were a pair of binoculars, a sextant, a compass, a barometer, and some charts. Otherwise, they would have to rely on their wits. As the six men set off on April 24 and waved farewell to their colleagues on land, they knew this might be the last time they saw them. For those left behind, watching the *James Caird* reduced to a tiny speck amid the eerie magnificence of the ice pack, it must have seemed that they had only a small chance of survival.

Three days away from Elephant Island, the rescue crew encountered their first gale. As the spray flew over the sides, the canvas deck began to sag and seawater trickled down into the boat. Soon all of their clothing and their reindeer-skin sleeping bags were sodden, and after a few days their skin became raw from the constant chaffing. To add to their misery, as they crawled around the bottom of the boat on their hands and knees, their bodies became cramped with cold, and Shackleton became plagued by sciatica.

James Caird was a ship's tender, named after one of the expedition sponsors, and not intended for open sea. A crude canvas deck was tacked over her to keep the waves out.

Despite their personal setbacks, the men made good headway, covering 60–70 miles (96–112 km) a day. Accurate navigation was essential to ensure that they didn't miss their target and continue deeper into the Southern Ocean, because once they passed South Georgia, it would be impossible to tack back into the wind and waves in such a small vessel. Shackleton was

small and the waves were so big that her sails were emptied of wind as she dipped into the trough of the wave, only for them to be filled with an impatient flick as she climbed back out to the top.

It must have seemed very different from the last time they sailed across this ocean in the relative comfort of the 140-foot (42-m) *Endurance*, and the men were all too aware of their vulnerability. "We were a tiny speck in the vast vista of the sea— the ocean that is open to all and merciful to none, that threatens even when

> **"We were a tiny speck in the vast vista of the sea—the ocean that is open to all and merciful to none, that threatens even when it seems to yield. "**

fortunate to have a very good navigator, Frank Worsley, but even so, taking sights from a small vessel that is pitching violently in huge seas is a tricky business.

By the end of the first week, the boat was encrusted in ice, and the extra weight caused her to lie dangerously low in the water. The crew chipped away as much as they could, but she still seemed sluggish and low, so they threw the spare oars and a couple of sodden sleeping bags overboard. The boat was so

it seems to yield, and that is pitiless always to weakness," Shackleton wrote. "For a moment the consciousness of the forces arrayed against us would be almost overwhelming. Then hope and confidence would rise again as our boat rose to a wave and tossed aside the crest in a sparkling shower like the play of prismatic colors at the foot of a waterfall."

The little boat sped along with a will, and after just thirteen days at sea, the men spotted the black cliffs of South Georgia. By the end of the following

day, the 40-foot (12-m) cliffs loomed large as they picked their way along the coast looking for somewhere to land. By nightfall they still hadn't found a suitable spot, so they decided to wait until the next morning. Before the night was out, however, the wind changed direction and increased to hurricane force, threatening to drive them onto the rocks. The exhausted men, who had long since run out of water, had to ride the waves up and down into the wind for another two days and a night before they finally found a break through the reefs and landed at King Haakon Bay on the west coast of South Georgia.

Shackleton had deliberately landed there, even though he knew the whaling station was on the other side of the island, to make sure they didn't overshoot land. Now, however, they were faced with an arduous climb across the uncharted glaciers and mountains of South Georgia to Stromness, the nearest whaling station. Undaunted, Shackleton fixed some screws from the *James Caird* onto the soles of his shoes and, taking two men with him, set off for the final stage of their journey. Their thirty-six-hour trek, without tents or sleeping bags, took them to

4,500 feet (1,370 m) above sea level before they finally reached Stromness.

The next day, a ship set out to pick the rest of the rescue party at King Haakon Bay. But it would take Shackleton four attempts with four different ships before he finally managed to get through the ice floes to reach the rest of his crew marooned on Elephant Island. When he finally did reach them, four months after leaving the *James Caird*, he found that all twenty-two men had survived. After the tents had been shredded by 80 m.p.h. (130 km/h) winds, the men had turned the two remaining boats upside down to create more durable shelters, and they had survived mostly on a diet of penguin and seal meat.

It was to be Shackleton's last voyage to the Antarctic. After the war, he set off on the former seal boat *Quest*, intending to circumnavigate the continent by sea. But while the ship was anchored off South Georgia, he died of a heart attack. He was buried there in a Norwegian cemetery with the epitaph: "A man should strive to the uttermost for his life's set prize." His titanic struggle with the ice was over.

Shackleton and five crew left Elephant Island on April 24, 1916, to seek rescue. The rest of the men were left to fend for themselves.

Lehg II

Overall length
31 ft. 23 in. (10 m)

Beam
10 ft. 9 in. (3.3 m)

Draft
5 ft. 7 in. (1.7 m)

Sail area
454 sq. ft. (42 m²)

Designer
Manuel M. Campos

Year
1934

Interesting facts
Although bearing many similarities to the Norwegian rescue boats designed by Colin Archer in 1890–1920, *Lehg II* is said to be based on the whale-boats of the River Plate near Buenos Aires. The yacht was given a "modern" Bermudan rig (i.e. with a triangular mainsail) rather than the more traditional gaff rig (i.e. with a square mainsail) of the River Plate boats.

The designer Manuel Campos modestly reported: "I think I may say the result was satisfactory. The boat turned out to be fairly fast, stable, with a high reserve of buoyancy, easy to steer in all weathers; her owner and skipper considers her fit for navigation on the high seas anywhere and in any weather." During the circumnavigation, Vito Dumas suffered many injuries, declaring at one point that he would "never sail again."

His exploits were celebrated with special-edition stamps depicting Dumas as a national hero.

His aim was to be the first man to sail single-handed around the world without leaving the Southern Ocean. Within days of leaving home, however, Vito Dumas was contemplating another, far more gruesome, idea: the prospect of amputating his own arm.

An Ambassador of Peace

Vito Dumas (1942)

In June 1942 the world was at war. Russian and German troops were lining up outside Stalingrad for what was to be one of the bloodiest battles in human history, resulting in combined casualties of up to 2 million, and Japan was running amok in the Pacific. While all of these horrors were playing out on the world stage, down in the Southern Hemisphere in neutral Argentina, a 42-year-old gentleman farmer stepped on board his 32-foot (9.7-m) yacht and set off on the voyage of a lifetime.

Vito Dumas was fully aware of the significance of his mission and the poignancy of his timing. "A breath of panic ran around the world. It seemed that all was lost. All I had to do was stay quiet. It's so easy and comfortable," he later wrote. "What set me off, to throw off all my normal life and tempt fate? Was it to show that I was not lost after all, that dreamers propelled by their inward vision still lived, that romance somehow managed to survive? The young need examples; maybe, without being too self-conscious, I could provide one."

More than just a farmer, Dumas was an athlete, an artist, a writer, and a sailor. The son of a penniless tailor, he quit school early to support his family by working and painting maritime landscapes. He had won the championship of the River Plate when he was 23 by swimming the 26 miles (42 km) from Colonia in Uruguay to Argentina. He then became something of a celebrity in 1931, when he sailed from Arcachon in France to Buenos Aires in an old racing yacht—named *Legh*.

He had had *Legh II* built in 1934 with the intention of sailing her around the world, but a lack of finances forced him to sell her a few years later and buy a tractor in her place. Despite trying to devote himself to the land, however, he couldn't get the salt completely out of his veins. In 1942 he conceived a momentous plan: to be the first man to sail single-handed around the world via the "three capes"—the Cape of Good Hope, Cape Leeuwin, and Cape Horn—a journey of approximately 20,000 miles (32,000 km). If he made it, he would also be the first man to successfully sail single-handed around Cape Horn; the only other person to have tried it, Dumas' friend Al Hansen, died in the attempt.

Somehow, he had to buy back *Legh II*. A friend offered to lend him the money and others soon followed. And so his adventures began. By the time Dumas set sail from Buenos Aires on June 27, almost all his food had been donated—even the sails had been paid for by his former gymnastics club.

After a short sail across the River Plate to Montevideo, Dumas left South America on July 1. His timing could hardly have been worse.

sprung a leak. He bailed out six buckets of water and went to sleep. The next day, he bailed out twenty buckets of water, but by midnight the water was over the cabin sole. Despite the violent motion of the boat, he would have to shift the 500 bottles of drink he stowed in the bilge to try and find the leak. By the time he got to the front of the boat, where the movement was the worst, his hands were cut and bleeding, but he had located the problem. A plank had split and water was gushing in through the crack. He made a crude "tingle" out of a piece of canvas and some planking, sealed it with putty and red lead, and nailed it over the leak. By the time he had restowed everything, late the following day, his hands were raw and bloody. Having overcome his first major obstacle, he settled down to a fitful sleep.

The next morning, he felt a throbbing pain in his right arm and realized that it had become infected. The next day, the seas had abated, but his arm was worse. With both hands in bandages, he set the storm trysail and took the helm. He was 480 miles (770 km) east of Montevideo and 3,700 miles (5,950 km) from Cape Town. "There was a long road ahead and I had not forgotten to ask God for guidance," he wrote, "but I understand also that a seaman has to suffer and that the picture one sees from ashore, when fit and well, does not include the bitter realities of life afloat. I could accept these—whilst doing my utmost not to lose altogether the illusion of happier days."

By July 9 his right hand was swollen and misshapen and his temperature was rising. He decided to give himself an injection to reduce the fever. With the boat lurching to and fro, he struggled to hold on to the needle, which rolled off the table and had to be disinfected for a second time. The next day, his temperature was up to 104°F (40°C), and

A southwesterly "pampero" was blowing at 30 knots, and Dumas had to receive special permission just to leave the harbor. His boat had no self-steering gear (it hadn't been invented yet), no radio (that would have marked him as a spy), no bilge pump (he refused to fit one), and only one screwdriver. He had only one oilskin, which he wore over sweaters and several layers of newspaper to keep warm. As he waved good-

Exhausted after forty hours at the helm without food or sleep, Dumas lowered the mainsail and staggered down below to recover, only to discover that the bilges were full of water. *Legh II* had sprung a leak.

bye to his friends, he knew that his next stop was 4,200 miles (6,760 km) away, in South Africa.

Within a couple of days, the wind was up to 50 knots with seas to match. Exhausted after forty hours at the helm without food or sleep, Dumas lowered the mainsail and staggered down below to recover, only to discover that the bilges were full of water. *Legh II* had

all he could think about was the pain in his arm, and he realized he couldn't sit back and do nothing. Not only was the pain excruciating, he risked blood poisoning followed by a slow and agonizing death.

For the first time, he began to contemplate the unthinkable: amputation. It was something that had never been done at sea by a lone sailor, and it had the

potential for all kinds of complications, but soon he would have no other option. "If by tomorrow things had not improved," he wrote, "I would have to amputate this useless arm, slung round my neck and already smelling of decay. It was dying and dragging me along with it. It was septicemia. I could not give in without playing my last card." His next thought was: How would he do it? Although he had received several boxes of medicine in Argentina, he had no surgical tools and very little idea how to go about it.

Almost at the point of delirium, he said a prayer to St. Teresa of Lisieux and fell unconscious in his bunk. When he awoke several hours later, he became aware that his bunk was damp and wondered how water could be getting in through the closed portholes. Then he realized that it was pus. His 3-inch (7-cm)-wide wound had torn open, and the pus had flowed out of it. He reached for his knife and pried at the putrefied flesh to find the core of the

abscess. The pain was unbearable, but he had to get rid of the root of the infection before he could heal again. He then prepared a dressing of cotton and cicatrizing oil and bandaged the wound.

It seemed to do the trick. Dumas began to recover almost instantly. Within hours the sun came out and a favorable breeze sprang up from the south. Dumas set his mainsail, and six weeks later he arrived at Cape Town. He had the damaged planking repaired and three weeks later, set off again, sailing south of Australia via Wellington in New Zealand to Valparaiso in Chile before rounding Cape Horn. He arrived back in Montevideo on August 30, 1943, completing his historic circumnavigation in 272 days.

Elsewhere, the world was still at war. But in Argentina a gentleman farmer stepped off his yacht and completed the voyage of a lifetime. Dumas had achieved his dream and set an example of courage and determination that others would later follow.

The infamous Cape Horn, where gale-force winds blow 200 days a year.

Joshua

Overall length
39 ft. 6 in. (12 m)

Beam
12 ft. (3.6 m)

Draft
5 ft. 3 in. (1.6 m)

Displacement
12 tons

Sail area
1,560 sq. ft. (145 m²)

Built
Meta de Tarare, France

Year
1961

Interesting facts
Born in Hanoi in 1925,
Moitessier set sail from
Singapore at the age of 17 in
a wooden junk. After the boat
was wrecked on a reef, he
then built a 25-foot (7.6-m)
yacht, which he sailed to the

Caribbean. Unfortunately, this
boat, too, was destroyed, by
rocks. His book *Un Vagabond
des Mers du Sud*, became a
best-seller and established
him as an author and blue-
water sailor.

He built his new boat out of
steel and in 1963 sailed with
his wife, Françoise, to Tahiti
via the Panama Canal and
back via Cape Horn. His
second book *Cape Horn: The
Logical Route* turned him into

a hero. Of his eccentric
behavior, he says, "You do not
ask a tame seagull why it
needs to disappear from time
to time toward the open sea."
He refused to conform to
society's norms, saying: "I am
a citizen of the most beautiful
nation on Earth. A nation
whose laws are harsh yet
simple, a nation that never
cheats. In this [...] nation,
there is no ruler besides the
sea."

Despite his public image as a philosopher of the oceans, Bernard Moitessier was driven by some very private devils. So why did he opt out of the famous *Sunday Times* Golden Globe Race and instead travel halfway around the world to Tahiti?

The Dragon Slayer

Bernard Moitessier (1969)

It was on March 1, 1969, after 191 days at sea, that Bernard Moitessier finally faced his "Dragon." The Frenchman had signed up for the Golden Globe Race, but not without considerable rancor. Moitessier and others had been preparing independently to make the voyage when the *Sunday Times* got wind of the story and, by Moitessier's reckoning, had hijacked a pure adventure between man and sea. As if it wasn't enough to be the first person to sail single-handed nonstop around the world, the newspaper was offering a golden trophy for the first skipper home and a $12,000 (£5,000) prize for the fastest—providing they started and finished at an English port.

But when a reporter finally found Moitessier in his lair in Toulon, France, the sailor was far from being pleased with the news that he stood to win a substantial cash prize for a trip he was planning to undertake anyway. Moitessier told him that the proposal made him "want to vomit." "Such a journey, beyond time and right to our very limits, a voyage so fantastic, with so little chance of success, given what we were attempting, belonged to a sacred domain where the spirit of the sea had to be respected above all," he later wrote. "We didn't have the right to muck about in such a beautiful story with our grimy fingers, to turn it into a circus where a bunch of clowns would

set out to beat each other for money and a gold globe while the media pounded the drums."

At 43 years old, Moitessier had already lived an extraordinary life. Raised in Saigon, he was imprisoned by the Japanese during World War II and was later drafted by the French military to fight the Viet Minh after the war. He set sail on his own from Cambodia in 1952, only to be shipwrecked later that year. Undeterred, he built a new boat, which he sailed for six years before he was shipwrecked again, this time in the Caribbean. With these experiences firmly in mind, he built a new boat in 1961 made of steel that was nearly indestructible. Ironically, his voyage on *Joshua* from Tahiti to Alicante in 1961 and his book about the journey, *Cap Horn à la Voile* (*Cape Horn: The Logical Route*), helped stoke a blaze of interest in record-breaking single-handed voyages that would culminate in the Golden Globe Race.

But Moitessier's reasons for wanting to sail around the world were very personal and had little to do with any desire for glory or setting records, let alone winning prizes. Dissatisfied with the final chapters of his book and haunted by the suicide of his brother, Françou, many years before, he was on the verge of suicide when he suddenly saw a chance to redeem himself. He would undertake the "ultimate" voyage, sailing around the world single-handed, and

Troubled by past
failure, Moitessier
was battling with
his inner demons
when he set off on
the Golden Globe
race in 1968.

write a book so truthful that it would outweigh the errors of his previous, as he saw it, flawed attempt. The arrival of the *Sunday Times* on the scene with all of its prizes and media hype threatened to turn this personal quest into something far too public and one-dimensional for his liking.

Despite his reservations, Moitessier eventually relented and allowed himself to be recruited into the race. Whether it was the persuasion of the journalist, who had become a friend, or whether it

was his way of turning the situation against his media devils, isn't entirely clear. As he put it, "The rules did not specify that we had to say thank you." But it was certain that by the time he had started the race, he was flat broke, and the prize money would certainly come in handy. He therefore sailed *Joshua* up from Toulon to Plymouth, where he spent several days with fellow "competitors" Loïck Fougeron and Nigel Tetley preparing his boat for the journey. He set off from the United Kingdom

on August 22, 1968, ten weeks after Robin Knox-Johnston on the *Suhaili* and two months before the ill-fated Donald Crowhurst, who died during the race on *Teignmouth Electron*.

Moitessier's account of his circumnavigation is strikingly different from most tales of nautical derring-do. Instead of the usual accounts of howling storms and mountainous seas, we find the recalcitrant sailor philosophizing about man's relationship with the sea and the nature of God. Long before the days of

sophisticated weather programs, Moitessier used more rudimentary methods to predict the weather, including the stiffness of his tea towel—a stiff towel indicated low humidity and winds from the south, while a droopy towel meant high humidity and winds from the north. He seemed to enjoy his month in the Southern Ocean, during which he did yoga naked in the cockpit, communed with his "eldest brother" (God to some), and—despite a restricted diet and enforced isolation—achieved "a kind of undefinable state of grace." And

Moitessier had already sailed around Cape Horn on *Joshua*, with his wife on board, during an aborted round-the-world voyage in 1960–61.

unbeknownst to him, he was gradually gaining on his main rival, Robin Knox-Johnston, who had rounded Cape Horn just two weeks before him. With another 10,000 miles (16,000 km) to the finish and sailing a faster boat, Moitessier could still catch him, and even if Knox-Johnston did get home before him, he would almost certainly claim the cash prize for the fastest circumnavigation. Either way, there was still everything to strive for.

Just around the corner, however, lurked his demons. "When I reached the Atlantic after rounding Cape Horn, all my senses picked up the fetid smell of the Dragon. The stink came from the north, in gusts," he wrote. The source of the "stink" was clear: the *Sunday Times*, the media circus, and the financial inducements that awaited him in "the snake pit."

But to a man steeped in Eastern mysticism, the Dragon represented not just the outward evils but also the inner conflicts and the potential for self-destruction that was very familiar to Moitessier. "I would find myself caught in a web of contradictions spun by the Dragon, who was waiting at the finish line to fight me on his own ground, ready to use every dirty trick he knew," he said.

To understand Moitessier's next move, you have to relate to his state of mind. He was a man who had been tormented by inner doubts and by guilt. He had already escaped his past in Cambodia by sailing away from it, and he did it again at the start of this race. The sea had welcomed him to her bosom, cast his Dragon aside, and made him feel whole again. All that awaited him in Europe were "false gods," things that he didn't value, such as fame and money, while at sea he had found what he craved most: inner peace. And from the outset his venture had been more about the inner journey than any outward achievement.

On March 1, 1969, approximately 7,500 miles (12,000 km) from the finish, Moitessier changed his course and headed east. He headed back past the Cape of Good Hope, back into the Indian Ocean, back past

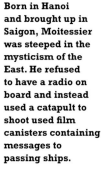

Born in Hanoi and brought up in Saigon, Moitessier was steeped in the mysticism of the East. He refused to have a radio on board and instead used a catapult to shoot used film canisters containing messages to passing ships.

Australia, back into the Pacific, and eventually, 13,000 miles (20,900 km) later, back to Tahiti. It was a decision that would shock the sailing world and the media, which immediately began to speculate about his mental state. His perfunctory message to his agent—delivered, in inimitable Moitessier style, by slingshot to a passing ship—hardly helped. It stated simply: "I am continuing nonstop toward the Pacific Islands because I am happy at sea, and perhaps also to save my soul."

> **"I am continuing nonstop toward the Pacific Islands because I am happy at sea, and perhaps also to save my soul."**

By the time he reached Tahiti, nearly four months after rounding Cape Horn, he had sailed around the world one and a half times and set a record for the longest nonstop single-handed journey at sea. And he did it in less time than Knox-Johnston took to complete one loop. The book he wrote about the journey, *La Longue Route* (*The Long Way*), went on to become a maritime literature classic and enabled him to live for many years in his beloved Pacific, where he became a passionate advocate of environmental causes. And as for his Dragon, it seems that the *Sunday Times* and the media were more easily vanquished than Moitessier's inner demons. It would be another twenty years and another book before he would put those ghosts to rest.

Peace, it seems, would only really come to him on the high seas and not in the pages of a book.

"My real log is written in the sea and sky; it can't be photographed and given to others," he wrote. "It has gradually come to life out of all that has surrounded us for months: the sounds of water on the hull, the sounds of wind gliding on the sails, the silences full of secret things between my boat and me."

His decision to keep sailing east instead of facing the media circus in Europe made him a hero to many—and turned him into an antiestablishment guru.

Perie Banou

Overall length
33 ft. 7 in. (10.2 m)

Waterline length
24 ft. 2 in. (7.5 m)

Beam
10 ft. 1 in. (3.1 m)

Draft
5 ft. 10 in. (1.8 m)

Displacement
9,195 lb (4,180 kg)

Sail area
650 sq. ft. (60.42 m²)

Designer
Sparkman & Stephens

Year
1973

Interesting facts
The farther south you go, the smaller the Earth's circumference and the faster it is to sail around the world.

The circumference of the Earth at the equator is 24,809 miles (39,924 km).

The circumference of the Earth at latitude 40 is 19,102 miles (30,740 km).

The circumference of the Earth at latitude 60 is 12,482 miles (20,087 km). To qualify for a round-the-world record, a vessel must therefore cross the equator twice.

Before sailing, Sanders was a wool classer-shearing contractor, working in a shearing team, then owning one for seventeen years. While away sailing, he kept himself entertained by reading and watching movies until the television set broke. Ironically, despite being at sea for so long, he didn't manage to catch much fish, although he had many opportunities for practice.

If he had been born fifteen years earlier, Jon Sanders would have been knighted by now. As it was, even a double circumnavigation barely raised an eyebrow in the cold North, and he had to take unusual measures to finally put himself on the map.

Three Times a Hero

Jon Sanders (1986)

When Robin Knox-Johnston completed his epic circumnavigation in 1969, wives, girlfriends, and mothers around the world breathed a sigh of relief. At last all of the great "firsts" had been done and they didn't have to worry so much about their husbands, boyfriends, and sons setting off on a wild scheme just to try and get their names in the *Guinness Book of World Records*. Or so they thought. Except that life isn't quite that easy, as Maureen Blyth discovered. While her husband Chay crashed around the house like a bear with a sore head, furious at losing the record to Knox-Johnston, she observed that no one had yet done it the "wrong way" around. The next thing she knew, her headstrong hubby was sailing his way around the world to claim his own "first," coming home 292 days later to claim his Commander of the British Empire award.

Six years later, on the other side of the world, in Perth, Australia, someone made the mistake of saying to yachtsman Jon Sanders, "You're too late, mate, it's all been done. There aren't any more "firsts" to be had." Sanders, a quiet, reflective man, thought for a moment and replied, "Oh, yes, there is: You can go around twice." That day, back at the Sanders family home, Jon's mother Dorothy shed a tear.

Sanders was certainly well qualified for this madcap adventure. Obsessed with boats since primary school, in 1973 he joined together with his family to buy a new 34-foot (10-m) Sparkman & Stephens sloop to indulge in his passion. Named after an Arabian princess, *Perie Banou* was a sistership to *Morning Cloud*, the yacht in which the British prime-minister-to-be Edward Heath won the 1969 Sydney-to-Hobart race. Sanders certainly put the boat to good use, sailing her around the world in 1975–77 to make her the first Australian yacht to complete a circumnavigation. Two years later he took part in the Parmelia race from Plymouth to Fremantle, set up as part of Western Australia's 150th anniversary celebration, and finished second overall. By the time he set off on his double loop, he had already sailed 70,000 miles (112,650 km) on *Perie Banou*, including 15,000 miles (24,000 km) on his own. And by his own estimation had probably made more race starts than any other skipper in Western Australia.

Sanders' record attempt, started on September 6, 1981, and completed on October 31, 1982, was certainly one of the most remarkable journeys ever made. Before leaving, he was fortunate to receive a sponsorship deal from Perth businessman Kevin Parry, who would go on to fund Australia's 1987 America's Cup campaign. Parry agreed to give him U.S. $12,500 (AUS $16,000) in return for printing his company's name on *Perie Banou*'s hull.

The 34-foot (10-m) *Perie Banou* had already sailed around the world once, but she was too small to contain all the stores needed for a 420-day voyage. Sanders's solution to the problem was widely criticized, forcing him to go one better.

Sanders's second boat was 11 feet (3.4 m) longer than *Perie Banou* and could hold enough provisions to last him for more than two years at sea.

On each circumnavigation, Sanders encountered his fair share of bad weather and suffered the usual knockdowns and equipment failure. By the time he arrived back in Fremantle 420 days later, he had sailed 48,000 miles (77,240 km) nonstop—twice as much as either Knox-Johnston or Blyth.

Sanders's achievement made him as famous as his British predecessors, and he was subsequently presented the prestigious Chichester Award and awarded an Order of the British Empire by the Queen. *The Guinness Book of World Records* ratified twelve records set or broken during the voyage, including the first person to continuously sail single-handed twice around the world.

But the sailing community—at least in the Northern Hemisphere—seemed unconvinced, and this speculation was based on food. *Perie Banou* was simply too small to contain all of the supplies Sanders needed to survive for fourteen months at sea—this was in the days before freeze-dried foods—so Sanders had arranged for his yacht to be reprovisioned at two points: in Tasmania during his first circumnavigation, then in Plymouth during his second loop. On neither

occasion did *Perie Banou* drop an anchor or stop moving, nor did Sanders get off his boat—although a few overenthusiastic journalists couldn't resist climbing on board to interview him during the Tasmanian transfer. Many in the yachting fraternity regarded this arrangement as receiving outside assistance, however, and refused to accept Sanders's record, dismissing the whole event as a gimmick.

Sanders then compounded his faux pas by writing a book about the voyage, which did not contain either the understated heroism of Knox-Johnston or the larger-than-life charisma of Blyth. Basically, he had made it look too easy.

But if the critics thought they could brush Sanders aside with such nitpicking, they had underestimated their man. Back home in Perth, it wasn't long before the lone navigator contemplated what to do next. Once again he was faced with the thought that all the firsts had already been achieved, and he realized that he could go one better. If Knox-Johnston had been around the world once nonstop and he had done it twice, then surely the next step would be to go around once more. Yes, he would circumnavigate the world single-handed nonstop three times! And this time, just so that there would be no question about qualifying for the record, he would carry his own food for the entire journey. There would be no stopping, restocking, or quibbling.

First, however, he would need to find a boat with enough space to store provisions to last him up to two years. The solution was a rugged 62-foot (13.8-m) sloop built in 1978 and renamed *Parry Endeavour* in honor of his loyal sponsor. To prepare the yacht for three consecutive assaults on Cape Horn, the bow of the boat was reinforced with extra layers of fiberglass, a new keel was fitted, and all of the rigging doubled. She also carried three heavy-duty mainsails, three general-purpose foresails, and a variety of other, light weather sails—Sanders wasn't taking any chances.

An armada of well-wishers escorted *Parry Endeavour* out of Fremantle on May 25, 1986, as she set off on her extraordinary voyage. For the first two loops Sanders sailed from west to east, but for the last one he turned around south of Fremantle and sailed the other way around, against the prevailing winds and currents, "to break the monotony." With each loop, he took a long leg up the Atlantic to just north of the equator to make sure he qualified for the record. Ever the competent sailor, Sanders once again overcame all adversities—including a close encounter with a fishing trawler off the Falkland Islands—to complete the voyage without a major incident.

By the time he sailed into Fremantle to a hero's welcome on August 20, 1988, he had been at sea for

It was only then that he discovered that just a few weeks earlier his father and, shortly after, his mother had died. He hadn't seen them for more than two years. It was a heavy price to pay to achieve his record.

Sanders's accomplishment won him numerous plaudits—including fifteen new entries in *The Guinness Book of World Records*—and it made him a household name in Australia. Both *Perie Banou* and *Parry Endeavour* were acquired by the Western Australia Maritime Museum, where they are currently exhibited as proud emblems of Australian maritime history. Sanders's triple circumnavigation was ratified by the U.K.-based World Sailing Speed Record Council, and his name stands alongside other giants of the sailing world, such as Slocum, Knox-Johnston, and Blyth. Jon's mother, Dorothy, would have been proud.

Although awarded an Order of the British Empire for his first epic voyage, Sanders fell into relative obscurity outside Australia after his triple loop.

By the time he sailed into Fremantle to a hero's welcome on August 20, 1988, he had been at sea for 657 days and covered 80,000 miles (128,741 km) single-handed and nonstop—two and a half times the distance covered by Knox-Johnston and Blyth.

657 days and covered 80,000 miles (128,741 km) single-handed and nonstop—two and a half times the distance covered by Knox-Johnston and Blyth. But the trip was not without its painful moments. A few days before the finish at Fremantle, Sanders, who decided early on not to receive any mail or messages from the outside world, called to shore to announce his arrival.

Groupe LG

Overall length
61 ft. (18.6 m)

Waterline length
58 ft. (17.8 m)

Beam
17 ft. (5.3 m)

Draft
12 ft. (3.75 m)

Displacement
12 tons

Sail area
5,059 sq. ft. (470 m²)

Designer
Bouvet-Petit

Year
1989

Interesting facts
De Broc says, "I think you achieve success in the Vendée Globe with a fast boat, an organized shore team and a skipper capable of imagining and enduring the challenges the race imposes. I haven't changed anything in my life for this. The main thing is to feel good in yourself. If, after three days, you feel like going home, don't even thinking about winning. You're done for. I am entering the race to win, but my main concern will be not to break anything."

This last sentiment is a worthy aim to have. In this second edition of the Vendée Globe race, five people did not finish due to lack of sufficient preparation or problems with their boats, including problems with keels, rigging, a lost rudder, and sails. Two sailors drowned, including one who didn't even make it to the start; he was lost at sea on the way to the race.

Single-handed sailors have to be everything: sailors, navigators, mechanics, riggers, and cooks. Sometimes they even have to be surgeons, too, as the French skipper Bertrand de Broc discovered deep in the Southern Ocean.

A Stitch in Time...

Bertrand de Broc (1993)

It was January 8 1993, deep in the Southern Ocean, and Bertrand de Broc had good reason to be pleased with himself. The French skipper was sailing in the second edition of the Vendée Globe single-handed round-the-world race, and as he ripped along halfway between South Africa and Australia, everything seemed to be going his way. After a chaotic and tragic start in which two competitors drowned and another six were forced back into the harbor, the only two skippers to have really hit their stride were de Broc on his yacht *Groupe LG* and Alain Gautier on *Bagages Superieur*. As they raced down the Atlantic, Gautier took the advantage and eased ahead, but nearly seven weeks after the start, de Broc had managed to reduce his deficit to just 280 miles (450 km)—not a huge distance in a 25,000-mile (40,200-km) race.

Birds were flying overhead, signaling that he was passing near the barren and isolated Kerguelen Islands in the southern Indian Ocean. The sky darkened, and *Groupe LG* heeled over as a sudden gust of wind caught her sails. A squall arrived out of nowhere.

Before de Broc had time to react, the boat was flat on her side and the sails were shaking with the force of the wind. The mainsail sheet was flailing about wildly, and it struck him on the head with such force that he was knocked unconscious in the cockpit. When he regained consciousness a few minutes later, his first priority was to get things back under control. Then, with the sails reefed and the boat back on course, he became aware of a bitter taste in his mouth, and he realized it was filled with blood.

Down below, sitting at the chart table, de Broc took out a small mirror and checked the damage. He winced as he saw a large gash toward the front of his tongue. It was still oozing blood, and de Broc knew it was potentially serious. It was 6:30 P.M. when he sent a message about the incident to his shore team in Quimper, northwest France. Each skipper had a logistics team and a communication center back home that was manned around the clock and had constant access to specialists— including the race doctor Jean-Yves Chauve. Because satellite telephones were not yet commonplace on yachts, however, de Broc could only communicate by telex and fax. "I've hurt myself," he wrote. "The top of my tongue is badly cut. Tell Jean-Yves. I'm bleeding a lot."

There was a 50-minute delay before his shore team replied, asking him to describe his injury. "Dr. Chauve wants to know whether the cut was made by your teeth," they wrote, "or whether it is ripped."

The new breed of racers introduced in the late 1980s had wide, shallow hulls with deep fin keels and were designed to take advantage of the following winds and enormous waves of the so-called Roaring Forties.

"It was made by my teeth," he answered. "The cut is about 1 inch (2 cm) long. It's 1 inch (2 cm) from the tip of my tongue and about 0.2 inches (5 mm) deep. It's not a pretty sight."

With 2,500 miles (4,000 km) between him and a decent hospital, de Broc's options were extremely limited. There might have been medical facilities at the Kerguelens, but even if he stopped there or anywhere else, he would automatically be disqualified from the race. The rules are categoric: No pit stops are allowed for any reason. All yachts are expected to be completely self-sufficient—and that includes medical emergencies.

Nearly two hours after the accident, he got the message he was dreading. "Bertrand, you are going to have to stitch it up yourself," wrote Dr. Chauve before giving detailed instructions of the procedure he wanted de Broc to follow. *Groupe LG*, like all the yachts in the race, had a comprehensive first-aid kit on board for such an emergency, and Dr. Chauve had

two or three knots in the thread. Make sure the two sides of the cut are in contact. You have to do it now, while the cut is fresh; otherwise it won't work and you'll have trouble eating."

Putting stitches in your own tongue in the comfort of your own home is bad enough, but having to do it on a boat in the middle of the ocean, with every wave sending the cabin crashing down with a jolt, takes a special kind of courage. De Broc's fingers were shaking as he took hold of the needle. He opened his mouth, looked into the mirror, and took a deep breath. As he pressed the needle into his tongue to make the first stitch, the blood, which he had previously stemmed with cotton, started gushing out of the wound again. The pain was agonizing as he forced the needle through the flesh, first down through one side and then up through the other, and then pulled the thread through. By now his fingers were slippery with blood and saliva and were shaking even more as he tied the first stitch. If he misjudged it and the knot tightened before the cut was properly closed, he would have to cut the thread and start again. He tied the first knot and pulled, and the flesh came together, oozing

Putting stitches in your own tongue in the comfort of your own home is bad enough, but having to do it on a boat in the middle of the ocean, with every wave sending the cabin crashing down with a jolt, takes a special kind of courage.

an exact duplicate in his office so he could talk de Broc through what he had to do.

"In the first-aid box there's a tray marked 1B," Dr. Chauve wrote. "Take out the packet containing the needles and thread—but don't open it yet. From the box marked 2C, take out the bottle of Xylocaine and the bottle of alcohol. Take out a compress, but don't unpack it. Wash your hands thoroughly with the alcohol. Pour some Xylocaine on the compress, press it on your tongue, and wait for it to take effect. It's an anesthetic. For the suture, use a straight needle—it's easier. You are going to have to put in two stitches, each a third of the way along the cut. Take a needle. Make sure there's enough thread on both sides of the eye so that it doesn't pull out. Pierce your tongue firmly and deeply, first on one side of the cut and then the other. Pull the two sides of the cut together and tie

blood. Then another knot and another. He leaned forward, blood pouring off his tongue, and checked his handiwork in the mirror. The thread stood out clearly: The stitch was good.

He took a deep breath and wiped the sweat, mixed with blood and saliva, off his face. His face was ashen, and he felt sick as he pulled out the needle to put in the second stitch. Again his tongue screamed with pain as he punctured its surface and forced the needle in, down, then up and out through the other side of the cut. There was a searing sensation, as if someone was pressing red-hot metal on his tongue as he pulled the thread through. Slippery blood-soaked fingers around tiny slippery thread. One knot. Two knots. And a third for luck. He stuck his tongue out again and looked in the mirror. His mouth was a bloody red gash, with four thread ends proudly sticking up. It was done.

"Okay, I've done it," he wrote. "Now I need something for the pain, and for my eye. I've got a bruise around my right eye and the eye is hurting, too." The message was signed "Rambo."

It was the first time anyone had to perform surgery during a Vendée Globe race, and the incident was immediately recorded down in the annals of sailing history. Later, in 1998, the Russian sailor Victor Yazykov faced a similar situation when he had to operate on his arm during the first leg of the Around Alone round-the-world race. But even that seemed almost bearable compared to stitching up your own tongue.

Unfortunately, while de Broc's courage impressed his fellow sailors, it didn't improve his fortune in the race. Two weeks later Jean-Luc Van den Heede, on Sofap-Helvim, slipped ahead of him into second place, and the following day de Broc received a telex from *Groupe LG*'s designers telling him they were worried about his boat's keel. Another vessel of the same design was found to have undersized keelboats and, even though *Groupe LG* had already made it halfway around the world, they didn't think she was safe to sail the rest of the way back to France. De Broc was forced to pull into New Zealand to have the keel checked, bringing his race to an abrupt end.

Although de Broc was forced to pull out of the race due to a faulty keel, his surgery was recorded in the annals of sailing history.

Aqua Quorum

Overall length
50 ft. (15 m)

Beam
17 ft. (5 m)

Draft
14 ft. (4.3 m)

Displacement
5 tons

Designer
Adrien Thompson

Interesting facts

Aqua Quorum was the only Open 50 in the 1995–96 Vendée Globe and the smallest boat in the fleet. The other yachts were Open 60s.

Up until 2004, the Vendée Globe was open to Open 50s and Open 60s, which competed on an equal footing. From 2004, however, Open 50s were banned. Open 50s and Open 60s are lightweight modern racing yachts whose design is "open," providing they comply to certain constraints, such as length (50 and 60 feet) and stability. The boats are mainly used for short-handed races, such as the Vendée Globe (single-handed), the Velux 5 Oceans (single-handed), and the Barcelona Race (double-handed). In 1988 Goss entered the 26-foot (7.9-m) catamaran *Cornish Meadow* in the Carlsberg Single-Handed Transatlantic Race, finishing second in his class. The journey set a record for the smallest catamaran crossing of the Atlantic from east to west earning him the Sir Alec Rose Trophy for an outstanding single-handed achievement. Designed and built in Cornwall, *Aqua Quorum* was christened by British TV star Joanna Lumley in March 1996.

For four years Pete Goss had dreamed of racing single-handed
across the Southern Ocean. When the time came,
however, he found himself entrusted with a far more important
mission: to save a fellow competitor's life.

The Reluctant Hero

Pete Goss (1996)

Pete Goss felt like a kid with a new toy. He had just entered the Southern Ocean, the wind was already up to 35 knots, and it was the first time he was in these latitudes on his own. He wanted to try it all out and see how it worked. The *Aqua Quorum* was cruising along at high speed, jumping from wave to wave, the hull slamming against the sea, its wake shooting up in the air behind like a plume. As she reached 23 knots, though, she dug into the bottom of a wave and almost jibed the main. Goss braced himself for the worst, but amazingly *Aqua Quorum* came up again and carried on as before.

It was a close one, though, and he couldn't expect to get away with too many more of those. Up on the foredeck he pulled the sock line to close the spinnaker. The sock came down 6 feet (1.8 m) from the top of the sail, then slid back up as the sail filled again. When the sail lost the wind, he pulled the sock line, farther down this time, until he felt something tugging at his leg. It was the lazy line from the sock, which had pulled it the other way, and wrapped itself around his leg. He couldn't close the spinnaker any more until he untangled it, but he couldn't reach down to do so without letting go of the other end. Unable to move, he clung on to the sock line for dear life as the spinnaker filled and lifted him bodily off the deck. He hung there, his left hand

burning with the strain of holding on to the line, while he wondered what to do next. It would have been a comical scene—the lone sailor dangling from the rigging in the middle of nowhere as his boat crashed on regardless through the waves—except that his life was on the line.

Eventually he managed to reach the spinnaker halyard, which hoists the sail up the mast, and ease it off until he was back on deck. He untangled the line around his leg and quickly stowed the spinnaker belowdecks before setting a smaller sail. He had learned his first Southern Ocean lesson and in future would be much more respectful of the immense forces at play in this desolate zone. After all, if something did go wrong, there would be precious little chance of being rescued out here.

Two weeks later, on December 22, 1996, it was his thirty-fifth birthday and he was fulfilling his dream: competing in the Vendée Globe round-the-world race. It was a dream that had been born four years before while he was skippering a yacht in Chay Blyth's BT Global Challenge. His moment of epiphany came when a wave rushed over the bow of the yacht and submerged him up to his armpits in icy cold water. "I wondered how it would be to return one day and sail single-handed on the lightest, fastest, most high-tech boat I could muster," he wrote. "I

wanted to surf down [...] to see how fast I could travel and discover what would happen at the bottom."

Farther into the race, Aqua Quorum had found her Southern Ocean groove. Although nearly 2,000 miles (3,200 km) behind the race leader Christophe Auguin, Goss had steadily made ground on his immediate rivals, Patrick de Radigues and Raphaël Dinelli. The attrition rate in the race was proving as high as ever, and of the original sixteen starters, six had already retired or were now sailing as unofficial entries, having had to seek outside assistance to fix their boats. Dinelli had been an unofficial entry right from the start, having failed to clock up the required mileage on his boat before the race to qualify properly. The quixotic Frenchman, at 28 the youngest skipper in the race, was already being referred to as the Pirate.

Now 1,400 miles (2,250 km) south of Perth, Australia, Goss was entering the worst storm of the race so far. As the wind built from the southwest, he rapidly reduced the amount of sail he had up: first the medium-sized number 2 jib came down; then he put a third reef in the main; then he took down the second foresail and raised the storm jib instead. As the wind rose to 45 knots, he took the mainsail down completely, followed by the storm jib, too, so that soon he was sailing under bare poles. And still the

wind strengthened—up to 50 knots, gusting 60. *Aqua Quorum* flew down a wave at 27 knots and crashed into the bottom in an enormous explosion of spray. Goss was doing what he set out to do four years before, and what he was discovering was beginning to worry even this most fearless of sailors.

Belowdecks his satellite communications system began to flash. He called up the message. Mayday, mayday, mayday. A boat was in trouble. It was Dinelli, the Pirate, on his boat *Algimouss*. He was stuck in the same storm as Goss, some 160 miles (260 km) farther back. Despite running under bare poles, the yacht was sliding uncontrollably down the 60-foot (18-m) waves. Dinelli had taken shelter below and had tried to steer the boat using autopilot. But the seas were too much. Algimouss went over and stayed over. The mast punched through the deck, and the boom smashed one of the cabin windows. Water started flooding the cabin, where Dinelli was trapped and fearing for his life. Three hours later the mast broke free, and released of its weight, the hull slowly righted itself. Only then could Dinelli set off his emergency distress beacon.

Back at race control the event's founder and organizer, Philippe Jeantot, and his team went into emergency mode. The Australian rescue services were alerted, and they immediately sent out a plane to look

for Dinelli. Nearest to the scene was de Radigues, sailing just 60 miles (100 km) or so upwind of Algimouss. But de Radigues had been having trouble with his electronics, and both his radio and telex were out of action. He sailed on by, completely unaware of the drama that was unfolding just a few miles away. The only other boat within range was *Aqua Quorum*,

probability, even—that *Aqua Quorum* might break up under such extreme conditions. But Goss's reply was immediate and unequivocal. "I had to go, I knew that. It was that simple […] when someone is in trouble you help," he wrote. "Not turning back, whatever the stakes, would have been a disservice to myself, my family, and the spirit of the sea."

> Up on deck, tethered to what was left of the mast, Dinelli watched his boat gradually sink beneath his feet. The life raft he had launched had broken free and was lost, so his only hope of survival was for someone to come to his rescue.

To make any headway against the wind, he would have to have some sail up, though, so he raised his storm jib and slowly turned *Aqua Quorum* into the waves. As the full force of the elements hit the boat, she was laid

but she was 160 miles (260 km) downwind, and sailing back into hurricane-force winds and mountainous seas would be like trying to swim upstream through the Niagara Falls.

Having failed to get hold of de Radigues, race control contacted Goss. Could he sail back and rescue Dinelli? As Jeantot made the request, he knew that he wasn't just asking him to put his race on hold, he was asking him to put his life on the line, because there was a very real possibility—

flat on the water, her guardrails and side deck submerged. Then, slowly, she recovered her equilibrium and, to Goss's amazement, started making around 8 knots' headway. She was sailing only at 80 degrees to the wind, but at least she was going in the right direction.

Meanwhile, a couple of hours after she had righted herself, Dinelli's boat had filled with water and was being kept afloat only by the watertight compartments that were built into her hull. Up on

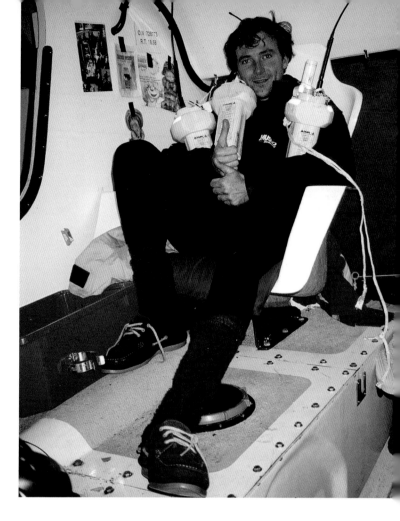

deck, tethered to what was left of the mast, Dinelli watched his boat gradually sink beneath his feet. The life raft he had launched had broken free and was lost, so his only hope of survival was for someone to come to his rescue. The storm continued to rage unabated, waves broke over the semi-submerged deck continually, and he felt his body temperature lowering. Christmas Day passed, then a freezing cold night, and then another day, and still he hung on to the boat for dear life. To avoid hypothermia, he danced up and down, shouting wildly at his boat, willing her to stay afloat just a few minutes longer.

Eighty miles or so downwind, Goss was having the sail of his life. *Aqua Quorum* was being knocked down almost every half hour now, and it was impossible to turn his face into the wind without having the breath knocked out of him. After twenty-four hours the wind eased to a relatively sane 35 knots (still a gale by normal standards), and he spent two hours repairing his mainsail so that he could raise it a little to increase his boat speed. A Royal Australia Air Force (RAAF) plane passed overhead and told him that they had found Dinelli and had dropped him two

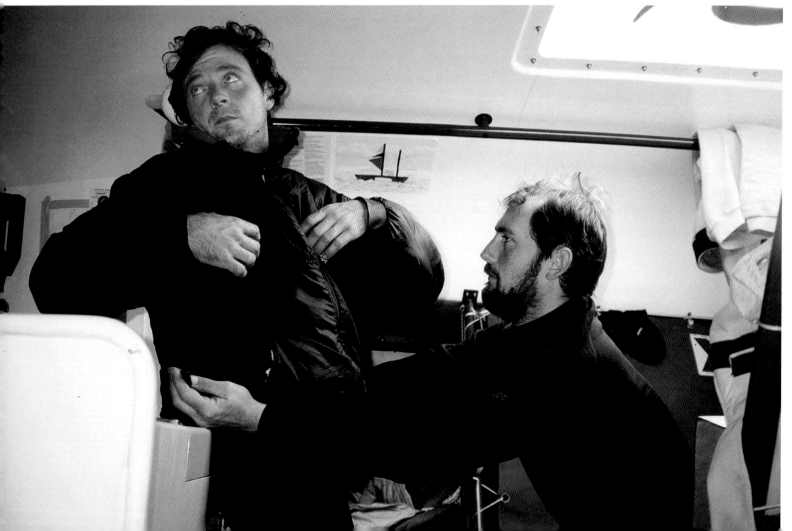

life rafts. It was just in time—minutes after the Frenchman stepped into one of the rafts, *Algimouss* finally gave up her battle with gravity and started her long descent, 3,500 feet (1,066 m) to the ocean floor.

As darkness descended on December 26, Goss was still 20 miles (32 km) downwind from Dinelli. Even with regular position updates from race control, trying to find a life raft among the waves in the dark was difficult. Every time a new position came through, Goss plotted it on his chart, tried to predict which way the raft might drift, and sailed up and down the track. And each time he found only more empty sea.

Finally, at dawn, RAAF rescue plane No. 252 flew overhead and spotted both Goss and Dinelli. Flying over the raft, they flashed their light to give the rescuer a fix. Goss took a compass bearing and pushed the helm over. As he neared the position, he lowered the mainsail to slow the boat down. Then he saw his target: a small orange blob on a furious blue-gray ocean. He streamed a line out behind *Aqua Quorum* in case he overshot the raft and, as he neared it, doused the storm jib. Two hands reached up to him, passing up spare flares, a box of stores, and unexpectedly a bottle of champagne. Then Goss grabbed both arms and Dinelli was on deck.

"The best Christmas present I've ever had," Goss wrote, "all wrapped up in an immersion suit."

Due to his exposure to the elements, Dinelli was frozen stiff, and it took several days for him to regain his mobility. Goss administered muscle-relaxant drugs and gave him some physiotherapy, and as they sailed downwind toward Hobart, a remarkable friendship developed between the two men. Despite the language barrier, they discussed ideas for boat designs and equipment and quickly established a rapport that would last far beyond the Vendée Globe.

The British sailor's courage didn't go unnoticed in the wider world, either. Goss was given a hero's welcome when he arrived at Les Sables d'Olonnes after 126 days, 21 hours, and 25 minutes at sea—finishing a disappointed fifth despite the time allowance given to him for his rescue attempt. He was later awarded the Légion d'Honneur in France and the Member of the British Empire in the United Kingdom, and his story was published in numerous newspapers and magazines. But what was perhaps most significant was his ongoing association with

Dinelli. The following year, they raced together in the two-handed Transat Jacques Vabre race, coming first in class, and later Goss was invited to be best man at Dinelli's wedding. A friendship forged in extemis at sea had developed into one for life, and the world had gained from their close brush with death.

Goss welcomed back to Les Sables d'Olonne by a crowd of 150,000 people. He was later awarded the Légion d'Honneur and a Member of the British Empire (MBE).

Exide Challenger

Overall length
60 ft. (18 m)

Interesting facts
Tony Bullimore is no stranger to risk. In 1986 his 60-foot (18-m) trimaran *Apricot* was driven onto the rocks outside Brest, France while waiting for a ship to tow her into harbor. Her lone skipper had to climb a 70-foot (21-m) cliff to escape a similar fate.

Bullimore's next boat, *Spirit of Apricot*, capsized in 1989, trapping its skipper under the netting in between the yacht's hulls. Bullimore's heart stopped and he was technically dead before being miraculously revived by his fellow crew.

The Vendée Globe race was founded in 1989 by French sailor Philippe Jeantot, two-time winner of the ROC Challenge, a round

the-world race with stops. All yachts in the Vendée Globe must sail around the world via Cape Horn without stopping and without assistance. The race starts and finishes in the Sables d'Olonne, in the Vendée department of France, which sponsors the race.

The deaths of two sailors at the start of the 1992–93 race ensured massive media interest in the next edition

in 1996–97. They weren't to be disappointed.

Approximately 15,000 people are thought to have climbed Everest and 448 people have been into space, yet only 163 people have sailed around the world single-handed, which indicates the level of difficulty in races such as the Vendée Globe.

The world held its collective breath for five days in January 1997
when a British skipper capsized in the Southern Ocean during a round-
the-world yacht race. A major air-sea rescue operation was launched,
and an Australian naval frigate set off on a 2,000-mile (3,219-km)
lifesaving mission. The question on everyone's mind was:
Where is Tony Bullimore?

Adrift in the Southern Ocean

Tony Bullimore (1997)

The Southern Ocean is one of the last great wildernesses on Earth. At around 3 miles (5,000 m) deep, it runs uninterrupted all the way around Antarctica and plays host to the strongest winds on the planet. Unchecked by any large landmass, huge waves build up and chase each other around the globe, usually accompanied by snow and sleet and near-freezing temperatures. For sailors it is a place of immense beauty and great trepidation.

Not that Tony Bullimore was thinking much about the beauty of the sea as he sailed his 60-foot (18-m) yacht *Exide Challenger* across the Southern Ocean on January 4, 1997. He was too busy trying to keep her on a straight course. The British sailor was three weeks into the Vendée Globe, the grueling single-handed round-the-world yacht race created by French sailing legend Philippe Jeantot. Problems with his fuel lines and autopilots meant that Bullimore had to turn back after three days and restart the race, which placed him 1,000 miles (1,609 km) behind the leaders.

With Cape Town now far behind him, a northwesterly gale was sending the yacht surfing down the giant waves at speeds up to 26 knots. It was both exhilarating and terrifying. Part of the trouble came from a "wing" mast, which, even with all the sails down, meant that she still carried a small amount of fixed sail. It was small enough not to matter in normal circumstances, but with winds up to 70 mph (112 km/h), it felt as if the boat was carrying a huge spinnaker that couldn't be lowered.

Eventually, Bullimore got the boat under control, and sailing at 60 degrees off the wind, he settled her down to 12–14 knots. Switching on the boat's autopilot, he climbed forward into the doghouse and closed the door behind him. Once below, he made himself a meal of corned beef on Ryvita biscuits and settled down in his favorite seat just next to the entrance. It was a safe place, where he could wedge himself in when the weather got rough and could still leap up on deck at a moment's notice if it was necessary.

Every now and then, as a particularly strong gust hit the boat, she heeled over until it felt as if her mast might hit the water. But he would brace himself and wait for her to come back up. It was during one of these rolls when Bullimore heard a sudden crack. The sound was, he would later write, "like someone snapping a fence post across their knee," And this time the boat kept turning, farther and farther, until she was completely upside down. Scrabbling to stop from falling over, Bullimore found himself standing on the ceiling of the doghouse. There, he waited for the boat to right herself. But as seconds passed and she refused to come back up, he realized that the unthinkable had happened: Her keel had snapped off.

With her light, easily driven hull, *Exide Challenger* was completely dependent on her keel to provide stability. Without it she would be unable to right herself or be steered in any direction. The boat would drift helplessly until she hit land, where she would gradually be broken up by the waves. It was every sailor's worse nightmare. "I could tolerate losing a mast. I could tolerate having my mainsail ripped to bits. I could tolerate losing a rudder. I could even tolerate losing steerage," Bullimore wrote. "But the keel is the almighty!"

He rolled himself a cigarette and ate a biscuit while he contemplated his options. Capsized 1,500 miles (2,414 km) southwest of Australia and 800 miles (1,287 km) north of Antarctica, he could hardly be in

"I could tolerate losing a mast. I could tolerate having my mainsail ripped to bits. I could tolerate losing a rudder. I could even tolerate losing steerage. But the keel is the almighty!"

a more inaccessible place on Earth if he had tried. But at least he was dry and warm, and he had enough food stored in the cockpit to last him several weeks. An eerie light came from the acrylic window in the ceiling and illuminated the tipped-up contents of the cabin. But instead of the blue-gray of early morning, it glowed green with the dim refraction of 3 miles (5,000 m) of icy cold sea. Overhead, he could hear the gale pummeling against the upturned hull, while below him the boom thudded insistently against the acrylic window.

Then, suddenly, a fountain of water erupted from the upside-down ceiling, shooting up to the cabin sole above his head. The boom had smashed the window and torn a hole in the deck, and the cabin was rapidly filling up with water. Now afraid for his life, Bullimore rushed forward through the engine room into the cabin and pulled on his survival suit. Next he set off his distress beacon. He then lashed the beacon to a length of rope, dove back into the doghouse, and pushed it out through the hole in the deck to make

sure it sent out an unobstructed signal. By this time the water was up to his chin—and icy cold. As the hull sank lower into the water, he knew he needed his life raft ready for a swift exit. However, the raft was in the cockpit, which was underwater on the other side of the doghouse. He would have to dive into the water and swim out to it. But first he had to open the door to the cockpit, which was pressed shut by the pressure of the sea. With the gale still raging outside, the flux and flow of the water meant that once the door swung open, it closed like a shark's jaw. Before he had a chance to enter the cockpit, the door had snapped shut on his left hand and bit the tip of his finger off. Stunned by the pain, he staggered back into the cabin and wrapped a bandage around the wound. But it was no use. As he tried once again to swim out to the life raft, the bandage quickly fell off, leaving trails of blood in the water around him.

Exhausted, he retreated back into the cuddy and dragged himself up onto the underside of a shelf—now facing upward—and he fell into a deep sleep. The shelf was just 18 inches (46 cm) wide and about 4 feet (120 cm) long with 18 inches of clearance, but it would become his place of refuge and the only dry place during most of his ordeal. And, incredibly, he always managed to sleep. "I'd squeeze up onto the shelf. I'd hurt my ribs getting there, and I had a soaking towel as a pillow; but all I had to do was lay down and say "sleep" and I'd go to sleep" he said. "I'm like that."

When he woke up several hours later, the first light of dawn was bathing the cabin in a green glow. Revived by sleep, he tried again to swim out to his life raft and, after half a dozen attempts, managed to reach it. He cut the retaining straps, but still he couldn't move it. The raft's buoyancy kept it pinned immovably to the cockpit sole. Unless the boat heeled over drastically, getting the raft out was not a possibility.

Although logic told him that *Exide Challenger*'s foam-sandwich construction meant that it was unlikely she would sink completely, Bullimore decided, as an option of last resort, to tie his remaining two distress beacons near the door leading out to the cockpit so that if the boat did sink, he could grab them on his way out. But the Southern Ocean wasn't finished with him yet, and while he was working in the doghouse with water up to his chin, the knife he was using to cut the ropes slashed a deep cut in the palm of his hand. This time it took an hour for the injury to stop bleeding.

At this point the water in the cabin was almost waist high. Most of the remaining food was sodden, and anything loose had been sucked out of the hole in the doghouse. All that was left was a tin of baked beans, a soggy Mars bar, and two sachets of water. There were still crates of food under the cabin sole but without the option of a life raft in which to escape, he couldn't risk flooding the lockers and possibly sinking the boat.

He had successfully managed to save his Survivor, a reverse osmosis water maker, and by placing one pipe in the sea and the other in his mouth, he was able to convert salt water to fresh water. It took about 500 pumps to generate half a cup of fresh water, but it was enough to prevent him from dehydrating—a very real danger, despite all the sea around him.

Because he was repeatedly submerged in cold water, the possibility of hypothermia was never far away. The survival suit Bullimore had put on after the capsize was made of 0.2 inches (5 mm) of protective layers, but he had left his full bodysuit at home and this one didn't have hands or feet—an oversight he quickly regretted. As the days went on, he could feel his body temperature lowering and he realized he didn't have long to live. On the third day, his fingers and toes started to blacken with frostbite, and soon after, he felt it spread to his nose and forehead. With no power and his food finished, there was little he could do about it.

He soon lost track of time and fell into a routine of survival. "Boredom doesn't come into it really," he said. "In the little time that you have got, you hold yourself together; it's hard to explain, but you are busy. You don't sit there twiddling your thumbs. In my case, I was either sleeping, or I was awake and doing a job, or resting. If I was resting, I was out of the water, and if I was out of the water, I was out of the cold."

By the fifth day the water was lapping at the underside of his shelf, sending small bursts of spray

Bullimore was racing to make up the deficit caused when his keel snapped off at the beginning of the race forcing him to turn back.

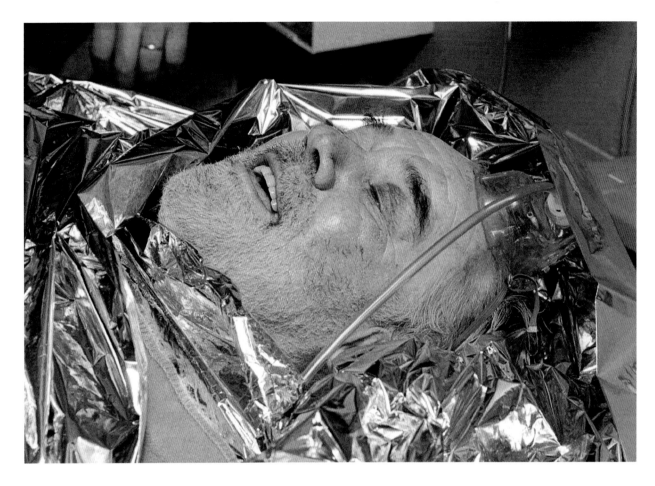

After nearly five days in his bolt hole, Bullimore was suffering from hypothermia, dehydration and frostbite—he eventually lost two toes due to the ordeal.

onto his face and making it difficult to sleep. As he lay there, drifting in and out of consciousness, he heard a loud banging on the bottom of the hull. Then he heard a noise that sounded like an engine. Jumping off the shelf, he started banging on the hull, shouting,

"In the little time that you have got, you hold yourself together... You don't sit there twiddling your thumbs. In my case, I was either sleeping, or I was awake and doing a job, or resting."

"I'm here! I'm here!" Sure enough, the banging came again, this time unmistakably man-made: "Da, da da-da dah. Dah! Dah!"

He scrambled out of the cabin, through the engine room, and into the doghouse, took a deep breath and dove down, out through the doorway, across the cockpit, and then deeper still to clear all of the rigging, and up again to the surface. In a few seconds he was outside—his first sight of daylight for

nearly five days. In front of him an enormous warship filled his field of vision. It was only once he was on board the ship that he realized the full extent of the drama that his capsize had unleashed. Unbeknownst to him, the only other competitor within reach, Thierry Dubois on *Pour Amnesty International*, had capsized in the same storm and had spent two days lashed to the rudder of his upturned boat before a rescue helicopter managed to drop him a life raft.

With no-one else nearby able to help, the 200-crew Australian frigate HMAS *Adelaide* was sent out to rescue the two men. But no one could be sure that Bullimore was still alive or even that he was near his boat, until a sonar device was dropped by a search-and-rescue plane. Beneath the sound of waves breaking and the rigging crashing against the hull, they heard a faint high-pitched noise, like someone clicking their fingers, and eventually worked out that

The two rescued sailors aboard HMAS *Adelaide*. The cost of their rescue sparked controversy in Australia, where they were accused of wasting taxpayers' money.

it was the sound of a reverse osmosis water maker being used. By the time HMAS *Adelaide* reached Bullimore, having picked up Dubois on the way, he was an international celebrity, and pictures of his rescue were in papers all over the world. It may not have been the kind of fame he wanted, but the tale of the "upside-down sailor" would be forever etched in the public consciousness.

Royal SunAlliance

Overall length:
92 ft. (28 m)

Draft:
12 tons

Interesting facts
Tracy Edwards was born in
Reading, Berkshire, in 1962
and raised in Purley on
Thames until the age of 14.
She went sailing for the first
time at the age of 7 when she
was sick for the entire voyage

and swore never to go sailing
again—a pledge she was to
repeat many times in her life
but never to fulfill. She was
expelled from school at the
age of 16 and worked as a
waitress on boats in Greece
before joining the
professional crewing circuit
in the Caribbean. She took
part in the 1985–86
Whitbread as a cook on
Atlantic Privateer, becoming
the first woman to win a leg of

the round-the-world race. Her
Maiden campaign in the
1987-88 Whitbread broke the
all-male stereotype and
played a crucial part in
introducing more women to
the sport. The following year
she was the first woman to be
named Yachtsman of the Year.
She was also awarded a
Member of the British Empire
(MBE) for her efforts.
   Edwards's crew on *Royal
SunAlliance* would all join her

on the *Maiden II* in which
they set a new twenty-four-
hour record, covering 697
miles (1,120 km) at an
average of 29 knots, and
broke their previously
claimed Channel record.
   Tracy Edwards organizes
sailing projects and spends
much of her time working
with disadvantaged young
people and using sailing
as a means of giving them
a second chance in life.

Not everyone welcomed Tracy Edwards's all-girl attack on the round-the-world record. When disaster struck in the middle of the Southern Ocean, however, the yachting world was impressed by her display of courage and determination.

Tracy's Eleven

Tracy Edwards (1998)

When Tracy Edwards announced in May 1997 that she was going to mount an all-female challenge for the Jules Verne round-the-world trophy, there were many that scoffed at her. A female crew wouldn't be able to cope with the rigors of the Southern Ocean, they argued, where brute force is needed to cope with the might of the wind and seas. At best she would give up before the finish and at worst she would be putting the lives of herself and her crew at great risk.

But Edwards was no stranger to scorn. Ten years before, her attempt to put together an all-girl crew for the Whitbread round-the-world race had been met with mockery, derision, a string of abusive phone calls, and even gasoline, being poured over her front lawn. Virtually no British company was willing to back her financially, and it was only thanks to the support of King Hussein of Jordan and his Royal Jordanian airlines that the *Maiden* project went ahead at all. Edwards and her crew of eleven women went on to win two legs of the race and finish in second place overall in her class—the best result by a British boat in twelve years.

The Jules Verne challenge was on another level, however. For a start it was nonstop, compared to the six-leg Whitbread race. The boat Edwards was proposing to sail was also in a different league to the

sturdy monohull she had skippered the first time around. It was the much-modified *Enza*, on which Sir Robin Knox-Johnston and Peter Blake had set a new round-the-world record in 1994. Now lightened by more than two tons, the 92-foot (28-m) catamaran was one of the fastest boats on the planet but would be far less forgiving than the *Maiden*. A catamaran relies on the innate stability of its width to stay upright, rather than on the righting moment of its keel, which is why it can afford to be so much lighter and faster. However, once a catamaran goes over, it has no reserve stability, so there's no going back. It's an all or nothing kind of sailing—ideal for breaking records but potentially catastrophic if things go wrong.

In truth, the doubters had good reason to be concerned. The path to the Jules Verne Trophy was already littered with failed attempts by far more experienced multihull sailors than Edwards—most notably the legendary Olivier de Kersauson who had failed four times before finally setting a new record in 1997 on his trimaran *Sport Elec*. By comparison, Edwards had no multihull racing experience before buying *Enza* and, once the boat was relaunched as *Royal SunAlliance*, she and her crew had only eight months to prepare themselves for the most grueling challenge of them all.

Her crew was made up of ten other women, all with sailing and technical experience. They were Adrienne Cahalan who had navigated on *Heineken* in the 1993–94 Whitbread race and was coskipper to Edwards in her later challenge on *Maiden II*; Emma Westmacott who had just finished racing in the 1997–98 Whitbread, Sam Davies who had just graduated from Cambridge with a degree in engineering; future round-the-world yachtswoman Emma Sanderson (née Richards) who at 23 was the youngest of the crew; the Olympic dinghy sailor Sharron Ferris; Helena Darvelid, who held the Round Britain & Ireland record on *Lakota*; Miranda Merron, an international 14 champion; solo sailor Frédérique Brulé; Hannah Harwood, the U.K. Women's Match Racing champion; and Miki Von Koskull who would go on to crew *Playstation*, one of the yachts designed for the 2000 round-the-world race, simply called The Race.

In the lead-up to the big event, the *Royal SunAlliance* team had mixed results. They failed to set a new transatlantic record but succeeded in setting a new cross-Channel record with a scorching 22.7-knot average speed. As far as their critics were concerned, it was all immaterial until they reached the Southern Ocean. Finally, on February 3, 1998, they crossed the starting line off Ushant in northwest France and headed down the Atlantic. Their target was the 71 day, 14 hour, and 22 minute record, set by de Kersauson the year before, and as they approached the equator, they crept steadily ahead of *Sport Elec*'s hypothetical position. Back on land, de Kersauson was unimpressed.

"I am confident that even if the girls have been quite good until now and using the best of really imperfect weather conditions, my opinion is that the trimaran is a better all-round boat than a catamaran," he was quoted as saying. "We will be faster in the Southern Ocean. We own all the ocean records between Good Hope and Cape Horn. I wish the

As with her previous crew on the *Maiden*, many of the sailors Edwards gathered on *Royal SunAlliance* went on to become successful sailors in their own right.

best of luck to the girls, but I don't see any reason why they will catch *Sport Elec*."

In fact, de Kersauson was just about to lose one of his precious records. Despite falling behind after passing the equator, *Royal SunAlliance* found her groove in the Southern Ocean and hurtled past Tasmania at an average of 21 knots. The gap between them and *Sport Elec* narrowed once more, and two days later, they snatched the Australia to New Zealand record. It was vindication that even a "girl" crew could race in the Southern Ocean and win.

By now Edwards and her team were in full flight chasing *Sport Elec*'s record. None of them had sailed

By now, Edwards and her team were in full flight chasing *Sport Elec*'s record. None of them had sailed the Southern Ocean on a catamaran, but they were soon squeezing every ounce of velocity out of their nervy speedster.

the Southern Ocean on a catamaran, but they were soon squeezing every ounce of velocity out of their nervy speedster. *Royal SunAlliance* surfed down the 30-foot (9-m) waves as if her life depended on it,

hitting top speeds of up to 39 knots and often averaging up to 20 knots. The boat and her crew were being pushed to their limit, however, and both were showing the strain. The catamaran's hull flexed alarmingly where the internal framework was beginning to come adrift and tell tale cracks started spreading on the so-called God Pod accommodation module in between the two hulls. Edwards was overcome by seasickness and then discovered the first stages of frostbite on her feet, while other members of the crew were suffering from a variety of injuries.

At the same time the boat was being forced farther and farther south by the angle of the wind—closer and closer to icebergs. Only the threat of a massive depression approaching from the west and threatening 70-knot winds finally forced Edwards to back down and head north to the relative safety of 52 degrees south. It meant losing a few precious miles to *Sport Elec*, but with winds already reaching 60 knots and waves up to 50 feet (15 m) high she knew she had no choice. Below decks, in the privacy

Many people were skeptical about the all-female team that had been put together, but they silenced their critics and gained the respect of the sailing world.

Catamarans are usually faster than monohulls but have less stability and are unable to right themselves. Edwards had no multihull racing experience, causing people to doubt her capabilities for the task she set herself.

It wasn't all sweat and tears. Edwards and her crew in festive mode during the voyage.

of her bunk, where she was confined for much of the time because of a back injury, she began to recite Psalm 27 to herself. "The Lord is my light, and my salvation; Whom then shall I fear?" In fact, she was as afraid as she had ever been.

When the end came, it came surprisingly slowly. A wave sent the catamaran shooting down into its trough at 30 knots and for a few split seconds she just hung there. Down below, Edwards and her crew

way up. The wind cracked the sails flat and the boat surged forward. It was several seconds before the waves exacted their full punishment as the mast came down, and even then it collapsed with a whimper, as it simply crumpled from the top down.

It was the forty-third day of Edwards's record attempt, and she and her crew had traveled 15,200 miles (24,460 km) since setting off from Ushant. They were now halfway between New Zealand and Cape Horn, and the nearest land was Antarctica, 1,200 miles (1,930 km) to the south.

"My heart felt ready to break... A thoroughbred racing catamaran had become little more than a floating platform. The easy option would have been to call the search and rescue services...But that was not in the spirit of the adventure."

were flung forward, while those on deck were flung to the front end of the cockpit. They knew that if the boat went over, there would be no way of getting her back up. She would just drift upside down like a raft. They would either be trapped inside or pinned under the netting that was stretched between the hulls. Instead, the wave passed under the catamaran, and she settled back in the water again, the right

As daylight broke, the scale of the devastation became evident. "My heart felt ready to break," Edwards wrote. "A thoroughbred racing catamaran had become little more than a floating platform." The easy option would have been to call the search and rescue services and hope that a ship might come and rescue them. But that was not in the spirit of the adventure. Instead, they cut away the mast and rigging, keeping a 21-foot (6.4-m) section, and let it drop over the side. Using wires and pulleys, they raised the remaining section of mast and hoisted the yacht's storm jib, sideways up, as a diminutive mainsail. Less than twelve hours after the accident, *Royal SunAlliance* was sailing again at around 9 knots—quite a respectable speed for a crippled yacht. Edwards's bid for the Jules Verne Trophy was well and truly over, and the best she could do now was to head for Chile, still some 2,300 miles (3,700 km) to the east, to make repairs or even, perhaps, to have the yacht shipped home.

It took them sixteen days to reach land, and as they emerged from the Southern Ocean and the wind faded away behind them, they took a tow from a tug for the final 400 miles (640 km). It was an emotional time for all of them as they came to terms with their shattered dreams, but a steady stream of supportive e-mails buoyed their spirits. Their determined efforts had not gone unnoticed by the rest of the world, and the talk of "weakness" and "inexperience" was replaced by references to "one

of the greatest sailing challenges of the past years" and of the record being "in their hands." The yachting establishment, it seems, had acquired a new sense of respect for this first Jules Verne "girl" crew. Famous sailors such as Pete Goss, Peter Blake, and Grant Dalton sent messages of support, and expressed their sympathy for what had happened. Then came a message written in French. It read: "The courage, determination, and seamanship that you and your team have shown during this Jules Verne trophy attempt does not deserve this horrible dismasting. We share your sadness. You have just completed a magnificent journey around the bottom of the world. Courage, respect, and friendship."

It was signed Olivier de Kersauson.

It was an emotional return home for Edwards and her team. Although they didn't win the Jules Verne, they did break several records en route.

Aviva

Overall length
72 ft. (21.6 m)

Beam
18 ft. 2 in. (5.5 m)

Draft
10 ft. (3 m)

Displacement
37.5 tons

Sail area
2,825 sq. ft. (262.5 m²)

Interesting facts
The first woman to make a major single-handed crossing was British sailor Ann Davison, who sailed the Atlantic in 1952 on the 22-foot (6.7-m) cutter *Felicity Ann*. Then in 1969 Sharon Sites Adams, from the United States became the first woman to sail solo across the Pacific, crossing from Yokohama, Japan, to San Diego, California, United States in

seventy-five days. But the round-the-world mantle remained unclaimed until the late 1970s, when a spate of attempts was made. Polish naval engineer Krystina Chojnowska-Liskiewicz made the first solo circumnavigation by a woman in 1976–78, although she traveled via the Panama Canal and received assistance on the way.

The first unassisted loop via Cape Horn was achieved

by New Zealander Naomi James in 1977–78.

The first nonstop circumnavigation was finally nailed by Australia sailor Kay Cottee in 1988—twenty years after Robin Knox-Johnston did it for the boys. The first "westabout" (i.e. "wrong" way) voyage was by Samantha Brewster in 1996, although she had to be "assisted" when her rig was damaged.

She'd already done it once with a crew of eighteen.
Now British sailor Dee Caffari was going to try to sail around the
world the "wrong" way on her own—and without stopping.
But the Southern Ocean had other ideas.

The Last Record

Dee Caffari (2005)

As the world entered the twenty-first century with its eyes firmly set on new horizons in space, most people assumed that all the great sailing "firsts" on Earth had already been achieved: first to sail around the world; first to sail around the world single-handed; first to sail around the world single-handed nonstop, first to sail around the world single-handed nonstop the "wrong" way, and so it went on. Strangely, though, one first remained unclaimed: No woman had sailed around the world single-handed nonstop the wrong way.

Only a handful of men have attempted what has been dubbed the "impossible voyage." Perhaps that wasn't too surprising. After all, by sailing east to west, sailors pit themselves against the prevailing winds and currents that flow across the Earth's surface as it rotates in a clockwise direction. Faced with relentless harsh winds and high seas, especially in the Southern Ocean, it is sensible to simply go with the flow—from west to east. The first to go in the opposite direction was Chay Blyth in 1971, who completed his circumnavigation in 292 days—a record that stood for a remarkable twenty-three years. Since then, there have been numerous attempts at the west-east record, but only three sailors have set new times sailing the other way, whittling the time down to the current 122 days. The only woman to attempt the journey was Samantha Brewster, who sensibly stopped off en route for a breather. The nonstop women's record was therefore still up for grabs.

Dee Caffari knew what she was getting into—or so she thought. As skipper of the yacht *Imagine it. Done.* in the 2005–06 Global Challenge, she had led her eighteen-member amateur crew around the world the wrong way. Despite retiring from the second leg after a medical emergency, they completed the race and even managed to get a podium place in leg six, the penultimate leg of the race. It was during the stopover in Cape Town, South Africa, that Sir Chay, who ran the Global Challenge, suggested she attempt the record using one of the Challenge boats. "The seed of the idea took root during the next leg and by the time I reached Boston I had decided I wanted to attempt it," Dee wrote. "During the last leg back from Boston, I spent time with my team assessing the boat and working out how to modify it for single-handed sailing."

By November 20, 2005, all the modifications had been completed and the newly renamed *Aviva* set off from Southampton. A week later she was buffeted by 72-knot winds off Portugal, and the following week, as she headed down the Atlantic, Caffari was forced to climb up the mast to clear a tangled line—a task every single-hander dreads. Even before reaching Cape

Horn, the viability of the voyage was thrown into doubt when Caffari discovered oil leaking from the autopilot and, for a while, she had to resort to using a dish towel to steer the boat!

But all of this was nothing compared to what was awaiting her in the Roaring Forties—so called due to the strong winds that blow in the latitudes between 40 and 50 degrees South. Like a bird being lured with no escape, Caffari rounded Cape Horn in near windless conditions on January 4 and entered the Southern Ocean. After nearly a week of benign weather and following winds, she got her first taste of what was to come as the winds shifted and resumed their more usual direction—blowing on the nose. *Aviva* was hit by a Force 10 storm, and to make matters worse, the autopilot malfunctioned, turning the boat so that the wind caught the sails on the wrong side. The vessel was pinned down for nearly 30 minutes, stretching

the rigging to the limit, before Caffari managed to bring it around again.

For nearly two weeks the yacht was pounded by westerly gales, never going below 30 knots and often reaching over 50. In a rare conversation via satellite with her shore crew, Caffari spoke haltingly and could be heard losing her breath as the yacht fell down wave after wave. While most sailors heading in the more sensible west-to-east direction would now be enjoying a fast—albeit terrifying—downhill ride, Caffari had to grit her teeth and sail into the full force of the storm. The result was a crazy, zigzagging course, tacking first to the south and then to the north, as she clawed her way westward across the Southern Ocean.

On February 3 she wrote: "Twelve hours of 45-knot winds with gusts into the 50s, mountainous blue-gray seas with wild foaming tops, which were being whisked away by the wind. Bottomless troughs that sucked you down, walls of icy cold seawater that broke and covered whatever was in its path. *Aviva* went from being a 45-ton steel yacht charging forward with purpose to being a cork lost in an endless watery landscape that was wild with fury."

A month later everything had changed. After 102 days of battling the elements, *Aviva* emerged at the other end of the Southern Ocean to no wind—and icebergs. Caffari was in one of the circumnavigator's eternal dilemmas: The farther south she went, the shorter the distance she would have to sail, but the nearer to Antarctica she sailed, the greater the risk of encountering ice—the one thing single-handed sailors fear more than strong winds.

Already exhausted from fifty-nine grueling days in the Southern Ocean, Caffari now had the demanding task of navigating a safe passage through the 'bergs. Glued to her radar, she couldn't afford to sleep for

> **❝Twelve hours of 45-knot winds with gusts into the 50s, mountainous blue-gray seas with wild foaming tops...*Aviva* went from being a 45-ton steel yacht charging forward with purpose to being a cork lost in an endless watery landscape that was wild with fury. ❞**

more than a few minutes at a time. Even then, any progress westward was blocked by the lightest of breezes. This forced her to choose between sailing farther south and risking more ice, or northeast—which would be backward. It was at this point that she wondered whether she could continue. "Utter despair took hold today," she wrote. "I sat for the first time on this voyage saying to myself, "I can't do this." I didn't even have the strength to cry at first, I was too tired for physical signs of emotion; there was just this voice inside my head."

Ten weeks later, however, *Aviva* crossed the "finish line" 1.6 miles (2.6 km) off the Lizard Lighthouse in Cornwall at 5:55 p.m. on May 18.

It had taken Caffari 178 days, 3 hours, and 6 minutes to travel 29,227 nautical miles and to become the first woman to sail around the world single-handed nonstop the wrong way. Finally, thirty-five years after Chay Blyth did it for the guys, she had done it for the gals, and the last great sailing first had been claimed.

Caffari's successful return, having captured the last great sailing first.

Hugo Boss / Ecover

Overall length
Hugo Boss: 60 ft. (18 m)
Ecover: 60 ft. (18 m)

Beam
Hugo Boss: 18 ft. (5.5 m)
Ecover: 19 ft. (5.7 m)

Draft
Hugo Boss: 14 ft. 7 in. (4.5 m)
Ecover: 14 ft. 7 in. (4.5 m)

Sail area
Hugo Boss: 2,583 sq. ft. (240 m²)
Ecover: 2,798 sq. ft. (260 m²)

Designer
Hugo Boss: Marc Lombard
Ecover: Owen Clarke Design LLP

Launched
Hugo Boss: 1999
Ecover: June 2003

Interesting facts
"The master of a ship at sea which is in a position to be able to provide assistance on receiving information from any source that persons are in distress at sea, is bound to proceed with all speed to their assistance, if possible informing them or the search and rescue service that the ship is doing so. This obligation to provide assistance applies regardless of the nationality or status of such persons or the circumstances in which they are found."

From the *International Convention for the Safety of Life at Sea* (SOLAS), 1974, Chapter 5, Regulation 33

When two bitter rivals, Alex Thomson and Mike Golding,
set off on the 2006 Velux 5 Oceans Race, sparks were sure to fly.
But no one could have anticipated the strange sequence of events that
brought them face-to-face in the Southern Ocean.

Friend or Foe?

Mike Golding and Alex Thomson (2006)

It was no secret that there was little love lost between British sailors Mike Golding and Alex Thomson before the start of the 2006 Velux 5 Oceans Race. At age 46, Golding had already sailed around the world five times, including completing three solo circumnavigations, and in the process had notched up eighteen equatorial crossings. His consistent success in Open 60 yachts had made him champion of the International Monohull Open Classes Association (IMOCA) Open 60 class two years running. The one thing that had eluded him, however, was a win in a single-handed round-the-world race, and he was determined to rectify that this time.

Thomson, on the other hand, was a relative newcomer. At 32, he had already won one round-the-world competition, the 1998–99 Clipper Round the World Race, and four years later set a twenty-four-hour solo record of 19.5 knots during the Défi Atlantique Race from Brazil to Europe. He had a high-profile sponsor, the clothing designer Hugo Boss, and had an ambitious program—taking part in three round-the-world races in three years.

The pair had been snipping at each other for weeks before the start of the race, leading race director David Adams to describe them as "two randy bulls in a very small paddock." Matters did not improve when, during the in-port racing before the main start at

Bilbao, in Spain, Thomson, who was in the lead on *Hugo Boss*, deliberately messed up by sailing on the wrong side of the finish buoy. Superstition has it that whoever wins the in-port race won't win the main race. Golding, who was in second place on *Ecover*, didn't spot Thomson's ruse and, much to his disgust, ended up winning. But the final straw came when, in a newspaper article relayed to Thomson after the start of the race, Golding described his rival with an obscene word. The knives were drawn.

Six skippers set out from Bilbao, Spain, on October 22, but with 50- to 70-knot winds flattening the fleet in the first forty-eight hours, four of the starters were soon back in the harbor having to make emergency repairs to their yachts, including Golding and Thomson. By the time they had all restarted, the fleet was widely scattered; the race leader, Bernard Stamm, was already approaching the Cape Verde islands, while 1,500 miles (2,400 km) behind, the stragglers were just getting out to sea again. Somewhere in between, Golding and Thomson were almost neck and neck tearing down the Atlantic trying to make up for lost time, the IMOCA champion in front and the young upstart snapping at his heels. It looked as if Golding's years of experience were paying off as he caught up with second-placed Kojiro Shiraishi when, in a tactical move, Thomson

overtook both boats and bagged the second spot.
Even the dolphins gave *Ecover* a wide berth that day.

With Stamm out on his own some 750 miles
(1,200 km) ahead, everyone's attention became
focused on the very personal dual taking place
between the two archrivals. And sure enough, as they
jumped on the Southern Ocean merry-go-round, the
game of cat and mouse continued unabated. At one
point the two boats were almost within sight of each
other, yet they still maintained complete radio
silence—pretending that the other didn't exist, while
at the same time being aware of each other's every
move. Four days after Thomson had spectacularly
overtaken him, Golding took advantage of a weather
system to steal back a few miles and take second
place. Touché!

Often criticized for pushing his boat too hard,
Thomson tried to keep his cool as he saw his
advantage eaten away. By November 23 he was about
1,000 miles (1,600 km) south of Cape Town. He had
reduced his mainsail and set his small "solent" jib, and
Hugo Boss was making good headway, sailing at
18 knots in 35 knots of wind. As Thomson lay in his
bunk, the boat suddenly tipped over to one side. He
rushed on deck and freed the mainsail, expecting the
boat to right herself, but she just lay with part of the
mast in the water, her sails quivering like the wings of
a wounded bird.

Like many Open 60 boats, *Hugo Boss* was fitted
with an adjustable, or canting, keel that could be
angled up to 40 degrees—providing the effect of
seventy people standing on one side of the boat.
Thomson immediately tried to angle the keel to bring
Hugo Boss back up, but there was no response. He
went down below to check the mechanism in the keel
box, and his heart sank as he saw that one of the rams
that angle the keel had snapped off. This was a major
structural failure, and there was no way he would be
able to keep racing. It was now a question of survival.

First he had to get the boat upright. He clambered
over the tipped-over deck, pulled the mainsail down
and furled the jib, and *Hugo Boss* gradually came up.
Thomson then pointed the yacht downwind and,
under instructions from his shore team, jammed the
rams in place to prevent the keel from swinging. It was
just a temporary fix, however, and it only allowed him
to sail dead downwind—which on his current course
would take him to Antarctica. Slowly the reality of the

situation dawned on him, and he realized he would have to abandon ship.

Approximately 80 miles (130 km) farther west, Golding had noticed his rival's sudden loss of speed and suspected there might be a problem. He also knew that, as the boat nearest to him, he might be

First he had to tack *Ecover* back into the wind to reach *Hugo Boss*. Six hours later, in the middle of the night, he arrived and established radio contact with Thomson—for the first time in this race—and they agreed to wait until morning to make the transfer. At daybreak Thomson put on his survival suit, climbed into his life raft, and said good-bye to the boat that had meant so much to him. *Ecover* was standing nearby and preparing to pick him

After dismasting 1,000 miles (1,600 km) south of Cape Town, the former enemies had to patch up their differences and sail back to land under jury rig.

"It wasn't a hard decision at all...I was tasked with a new responsibility, and if it went wrong, I would never be able to forgive myself."

called upon to go to Thomson's assistance. It was a bizarre twist of fate, but when the call came from race control later that day, Golding didn't hesitate for a moment. "It wasn't a hard decision at all because a life was at risk," he said. "I was tasked with a new responsibility, and if it went wrong, I would never be able to forgive myself."

up. But a lumpy 15-foot (4.6-m) swell made maneuvering tricky. And to make matters worse, Golding's engine controls broke at a crucial moment, which meant he kept having to dive down into the cabin to adjust his speed. Meanwhile, Thomson was stranded in his life raft, slopping around in near-freezing water, knowing that if he did fall into the

Opposite: Alex Thomson was young and ambitious, and looking to add to his already impressive track record when disaster struck.

Hugo Boss at the start of the Velux 5 Oceans race in Bilbao, Spain. She was one of the three most competitive boats in the event but wouldn't make it to the end of the first leg.

sea, he would have less than five minutes to live. It took an hour of near misses before Golding finally brought *Ecover* alongside Thomson's life raft and dragged him on board. The first part of their ordeal was over.

It was a strange, almost surreal moment as the two men, who had done their utmost to avoid each other for so long and who just a few hours earlier had been locked in bitter rivalry, all of a sudden found themselves drinking coffee together. Before he had abandoned ship, Thomson's shore team had suggested that he take "a large slice of humble pie" with him when he boarded *Ecover*, but the advice was unnecessary. Thomson already knew he was lucky to be alive, and he knew to whom he owed his life.

"This has been without doubt the most terrifying and emotional experience of my life," he said from on board *Ecover*. "This yacht has been my life for three years. It's wrong to leave her down here, and I would have done anything to save her. But to be stranded in big seas 1,000 nautical miles from land, with an irreparable keel that was swinging uncontrollably, I really had no other choice. It was really distressing to look back and see *Hugo Boss* in such a sorry state. I am

hugely grateful to Mike for turning back to rescue me. He is a true, true hero."

But their troubles weren't over yet. Less than six hours after the rescue, *Ecover* was hit by a squall and Golding could only watch as her carbon fiber mast "exploded." Although half the mast was still standing, it would be impossible to make a repair at sea, and with the first stop at Fremantle, Australia, still over 4,000 miles (6,400 km) away, Golding decided to repair the boat as best he could and head north to Cape Town. His race was, in effect, over. Back on shore, there was a sense of disbelief that two of the top sailors in this prestigious event, both tipped as possible winners, had been knocked out before the end of the first leg. It was bad news for the Velux 5 Oceans, too, because with Golding and Thomson gone, there would be no one left to seriously challenge Stamm.

Strangely enough, the only people who weren't complaining were the skippers' sponsors. Thanks to the media obsession with football, rugby, and cricket, sailing events rarely receive much coverage in the general press. But a good, daring Southern Ocean rescue is a different matter—especially when it's

captured live on camera. And one thing the media-friendly Thomson had learned was to carry a camera with him everywhere. Even as he flirted with death in his life raft, the images of the rescue were sent via satellite to his shore team to be broadcast on that day's news. Suddenly, Thomson and Golding were hot news, and back in the United Kingdom they were interviewed by all of the national television stations and given unprecedented coverage in newspapers around the world. A documentary about the rescue was filmed, and Golding was awarded an Order of the British Empire for his heroism. The two bitter enemies were now an international touring combo, and they received much more coverage than if either of them had actually won the race. No wonder the sponsors were happy.

Golding was philosophical about the unexpected turn of events. "When you start a race, you never know what the challenge of that race is going to be," he said. "This wasn't the challenge I wanted, but it has been rewarding in different ways than I hoped or expected. So it is a positive story. Occan sailing, and ocean racing in particular, is a hard task master and you become fatalistic—if you're not already fatalistic before you start!"

Thomson, meanwhile, was having a new boat built for his next round-the-world contest: the two-handed Barcelona World Race. His coskipper for that event had been announced before the start of the Velux 5 Oceans, so it would be pure fantasy to suggest that he might sail with his new friend Mike Golding. But it would make a great story.

Alex Thomson, shows his gratitude for surviving a third potentially deadly accident in the Southern Ocean.

L'Oréal Paris

Overall length
85 ft. (26 m)

Beam
17 ft. (5.4 m)

Draft
15 ft. (4.6 m)

Displacement
29 tons

Sail area
3,660 sq. ft. (340 m²)

Interesting facts
In 2005 Fontenoy was named as one of *Time* magazine's European Heroes for her rowing voyage across the Pacific. "In an age when bored billionaires use hi-tech gadgetry to get their names in the record books," the publication said, "Fontenoy's feats hark back to a simpler time of personal strength, resilience and stamina—lots of it."

Fontenoy is an ambassador for the Nicolas Hulot Foundation, an organization that was created in 1990 by TV presenter Nicolas Hulot to promote greater environmental awareness. Five out of twelve candidates in the 2007 French elections signed the Foundation's "ecology pact."

The fastest, full east-to-west crossing of the Pacific by oar was by British sailor Jim

Shekhdar, who crossed from Peru to Australia (10,652 miles/17,142 km) in 273 days in 2000.

The fastest west-to-east crossing of the Pacific by oar was by the Frenchman Emmanuel Coindre, who crossed from Japan to the United States (5,988 miles/9,636 km) in 130 days in 2005.

When Maud Fontenoy set off to sail around the world the "wrong" way in October 2006, there were many who thought her "easy" route was a copout. It would take a disaster in the Southern Ocean to prove them wrong.

Around the World Her Own Way

Maud Fontenoy (2006)

It was the Golden Globe all over again. Back in 1968 it was the valiant British ex-merchant navy man Robin Knox-Johnston competing against the French quasi-mystical writer Bernard Moitessier to be the first to sail around the world solo and nonstop. Nearly forty years later we had the solid Dee Caffari battling her way around the world to be the first woman to go around solo the "wrong" way against the prevailing winds and tides, with the elegant Maud Fontenoy following in her wake a few months later. Their choice of sponsors said it all: Caffari had Aviva, the fifth-largest insurance group in the world, suggesting reliability and security; Fontenoy had L'Oréal, the largest cosmetic company in the world, signifying style and femininity.

Except that once again the French refused to play by the rules. Back in 1968 Moitessier confounded the world by refusing to sail back up the Atlantic after rounding Cape Horn and, instead, continued for another half turn of the world to Tahiti. By doing so, he abandoned his claim to the Golden Globe but somehow gained the moral higher ground by declaring that he was doing it "to save my soul."

The story was repeated late last year when Caffari romped home to Southampton, United Kingdom, after 178 days to claim her own record. A few months later Fontenoy set off from the French Pacific island of La Réunion on her own circumnavigation—except that she wouldn't be leaving the Southern Hemisphere. The world's media fumed as mileage claims were bandied about, and the World Sailing Speed Record Council was prompted to issue a press statement:

The WSSR states that the reported forthcoming voyage of Maud de Fontenoy is not being attempted under the WSSR Rules and her route has not received approval. Although her proposed voyage may have merit, it cannot be considered as an attempt on Dee Caffari's World Record … Starting in the Southern Ocean and then sailing around the Antarctic is probably a major achievement in itself, but as this distance will be around 12,000 nm it cannot be described as an Around the World voyage under the WSSR Rules.

According to WSSR Rule 26a, a vessel is required to sail at least 21,600 nautical miles (i.e. the distance of the great circle) to qualify as a round-the-world voyage. And that refers to the most direct route, not the actual miles covered, so when Fontenoy's press team argued she had in fact sailed 21,300 miles (34,280 km), they were quickly shot down by sections of the yachting media (even if it was true). For the purposes of the record, they insisted, she had "only" sailed 12,000 miles (19,300 km).

Fontenoy, determined to complete her circumnavigation under jury rig, turned down the offer of a safe passage home.

Yet when Fontenoy spoke to *Boat News* shortly after she completed her loop, she suggested that her critics were missing the point. She hadn't been trying to beat Caffari's record in the first place. "This was a personal challenge—a battle with myself, not against other people," she said. "I work a lot with children, to show to them that if you have a dream, you have to work to the end to make it come true. And not to let anyone tell you it's impossible. That is why I wanted

to sail around the world in the hardest way possible—against the winds and currents—to show them that the 'impossible' can be done. I didn't want to compare myself to other people, and I wasn't trying for the record. I did it just for the adventure." It's a sentiment of which Moitessier would have been proud.

Fontenoy was born in Meaux, France, in September 1977 and lived for the first fifteen years of her life on her parents' 55-foot (17-m) schooner,

other wildlife. Long-distance rowing is good for all these things."

She was to find plenty of strong challenges during her first record attempt: rowing across the Atlantic. During a storm-troubled journey, she encountered 30-foot (9-m) waves and capsized seventeen times in one night, but she made it from Spain to St. Pierre, an island off Canada, in 117 days, becoming the first (and so far only) woman to complete the crossing solo by oar.

> **"**Sailors can be big and bearded and very tough, or they can be small and feminine. And women do have advantages—like being more organized and persistent.**"**

For her next adventure, she chose the mighty Pacific. This time she had a trouble-free crossing, which she completed in just seventy-two days in January and March 2005—except that she chose to row from Lima, Peru, to the Marquesa Islands, a distance of 4,200 miles (6,760 km). That's about the same distance as crossing the Atlantic and more than 2,000 miles (3,200 km) short of the official Pacific record set by Anders Svedlund in 1974, rowing from Chile to the westerly islands of Samoa. Was this really a bona fide Pacific crossing? Could Fontenoy claim the title of the first woman to row across the Pacific? The media cynics were already starting to grumble.

Their grumbles may have had as much to do with the way she looked as what she did. Far from the "girls-pretending-to-be-boys" stereotype of many female sailors, Fontenoy was clearly all woman. "It's true I don't look like the typical sailor. I'm a woman, and I'm a feminine woman; I wear high heels and makeup. People do look at me strangely sometimes," she says. "But it's important to me to challenge that stereotype. Sailors can be big and bearded and very tough, or they can be small and feminine. And women do have advantages—like being more organized and persistent."

sailing on both sides of the Atlantic. Back on land, she worked for a few years at a real estate agency in Paris, but she always craved the freedom and purity of the sea. A chance encounter with France's leading long-distance rower Gerard D'Aboville turned her on to rowing and the challenge of ocean voyages. "I like strong challenges, things that require a lot of effort, because for me it's all about that inner voyage," she says. "I love to be close to the water, to see whales and

The French sailor says her sponsor, L'Oréal Paris, was a natural choice because of their shared interest in the rights of women and children.

Her next project was far more ambitious than anything she'd done before: sailing around the world nonstop. And she would need a major sponsor to make it possible. Her collaboration with the pharmaceutical company L'Oréal Paris was a coup de foudre, she says, because of their shared commitment to the rights of women and children. The boat she chose for the journey was none other than Jean Luc Van Den Heede's 76-foot (23-m) aluminium monohull, *Adrien*, in which he had clinched the outright "westabout" record in 2004.

Fontenoy's sound preparations of the renamed *L'Oréal Paris* would soon be overshadowed, however, by what was essentially gossip. Before she set off for La Réunion on October 15, 2006, an overenthusiastic press team made the mistake of describing her voyage as a first (which in a sense it was, since it was not the same "official" route followed by Caffari). The media got their knives out and laid into the unfortunate

sailor. As Fontenoy battled with gear failure and a broken thumb in her first week out, the credibility of her route was the hot topic on many boating forums. Even when she survived 60 m.p.h. (37 km/h) winds and 30- to 35-foot (9- to 10-m) waves off Cape Horn and nearly hit an iceberg, the issue of whether or not this was a record attempt dragged on.

Then on February 10, 2007, something unexpected happened. Some 900 miles (1,450 km) east of Australia the yacht's mast collapsed, nearly killing Fontenoy in the process. "It was only 30 knots of wind, much less than we were already used to. I was at the helm, and the mast fell very close to me. After four and a half months at sea, I think I was just tired. I was very scared. It was nighttime, and the broken mast was tapping on the hull. I was afraid of dying."

She launched her life raft, and as news of her plight was passed on by her shore team, the

international emergency services swung into action and diverted a German cargo ship to go to her rescue.

As day dawned on *L'Oréal Paris*, Fontenoy started thinking about those children who had written to her urging her to succeed, and she thought of her original motivation for the journey: to prove that dreams can come true. She started methodically cutting the mast and rigging away, saving the yacht's boom, which she then hoisted up to set a jury rig. It was a procedure that had been anticipated by Van Den Heede, who had ensured the boom could be locked into the mast step for just such an occasion.

By the time the cargo ship arrived, Fontenoy had decided that she would make her own way to the Réunion Islands, still some 2,400 miles (3,860 km) away, and finish her unconventional loop unassisted. Turning down the offer of rescue was a defining moment for the rookie circumnavigator—something akin to the moment when Pete Goss turned his boat

around in a Southern Ocean hurricane to go to the rescue of Rafaël Dinelli. It showed not only courage and fortitude, but, above all, a commitment to her personal beliefs.

It was another six weeks before Fontenoy sailed into La Réunion to an ecstatic crowd—largely composed of children who had been following her voyage via the Internet. The arguments about whether it was a record, or even whether it was being claimed as a record, rumbled on, but to most observers it no longer mattered. The young sailor had achieved what she set out to do and fulfilled her obligations to her sponsors and, more important, to the 20 million children who followed her around the world. What the rest of the world thought didn't really matter anymore.

Victory celebrations in La Réunion. Around 20 million children are said to have followed Fontenoy's progress via the Internet.

Arctic

Fram
Gjøa
Campina

Fram

Overall length
128 ft. (40 m)

Waterline length
113 ft. (34 m)

Beam
36 ft. (11 m)

Draft
17 ft. (5.2 m)

Displacement
402 tons

Sail area
6,000 sq ft. (557 m²)

Rig
Three-masted schooner

Built
Colin Archer, Larvik, Norway

Launched
1892

Interesting facts
Lines of latitude run east and west parallel with the equator; lines of longitude run north and south but meet at the poles. Every degree of latitude is divided into 60 minutes, each of which is equivalent to one nautical mile. One degree of latitude therefore equals 60 nautical miles. Because the world wobbles on its axis, the North Pole is not fixed. Various international bodies have come together to define an artificially 'fixed' North Pole for navigational purposes. The geographic North Pole is not the same as the magnetic North Pole—they are currently around 600 miles (965 km) apart. In Nansen's day they were more than 1,000 miles (1,600 km) apart.

It was the end of the nineteenth century, and the race was on to see who would be the first to reach the North Pole. The Norwegian explorer Fridtjof Nansen had concocted a plan that many experts dismissed as a joke. But this was no laughing matter: Thirteen lives were at the mercy of the ice, and a nation's pride was at stake.

Going with the Floe

Fridtjof Nansen (1893)

It seemed to be a preposterous idea: Drive a boat into the ice and let the currents and the movement of the ice floes "drift" her to the North Pole. Surely the ice didn't move that much, and in any case, what would stop the ship from being crushed like so many before her? The expert opinion about Fridtjof Nansen's proposal was almost unanimous: It was at best ill founded and at worst suicidal.

But Nansen had faced criticism before. When he set off to cross Greenland in 1882, everyone derided his plan to start from the unpopulated east coast and work overland toward the populated west coast. They argued that once his ship dropped them off on the east, they would have nothing to rely on if anything went wrong. And this was his intention. By burning all their bridges at the very start, he knew that he and his team would have to succeed in order to survive, and what better motivation? He was proved right, of course, returning to Norway in 1889 a national hero.

The great accomplishments still up for grabs at that time included the North and South poles, and with his newfound fame, Nansen immediately focused on claiming the North Pole for Norway. A few years before, he had read an article that described the recovery of relics from the American exploration ship *Jeanette* off the southwest coast of

Greenland. *Jeanette* was attempting to reach the North Pole via the Bering Strait, in between Russia and the United States, when she became trapped in ice north of Siberia. She then drifted for eighteen months in a northwesterly direction, *deeper* into the ice, before she was crushed and sank off the New Siberian Islands in June 1881. The fact that several artifacts from the ship had washed up in Greenland suggested that the ice had continued moving westward before being spat out into the northern Atlantic. While in Greenland, Nansen had examined pieces of driftwood, which he was convinced must have originated in Siberia and had been brought there by Arctic currents.

But the problem of building a vessel strong enough to withstand the forces of pack ice remained. For a solution to this dilemma, he turned to the boat builder, Colin Archer. The son of a timber merchant, Archer achieved some fame with a new double-ended pilot boat that was designed to withstand any weather. The boat he built for Nansen was unlike anything that had ever been built before or since. Nansen and Archer reasoned that the bottom of the ship would have to be completely smooth, with a rounded, almost egg-shaped hull, to avoid being crushed by the ice. So when the ice did bear down on the vessel, she would simply be pushed upward,

Fram was unlike any boat that had ever been built before. Massively strong, she was designed to withstand the pressure of the ice pack.

out of its way, instead of being destroyed. Or, as Nansen surmised, "The whole craft should be able to slip like an eel out of the embrace of the ice."

The boat would also have to be phenomenally strong. And Archer took no chances. The hull was 24 to 28 in. (60 to 70 cm) thick and consisted of two layers of oak clad with a layer of greenheart—a South American evergreen tree—all held together by massive oak frames. The front of the boat was stiffened with three oak timbers totaling 4 feet

(1.2 m), while the keel was recessed into the hull so that only 3 inches (7.5 cm) of it projected outside to prevent the ice from getting any purchase. Inside, a cobweb of beams and braces prevented any twisting. The ship also was heavily insulated against the cold and had a well-stocked library, plus games and musical instruments, to help while away the long Arctic winters.

Fram (Norwegian for "forward") sailed from Christiania (now known as Oslo) on June 24, 1893, and almost immediately ran into her first gale. Nansen and his crew of twelve men soon discovered that all of the things that made the ship suitable for the ice also made her very unsuitable for regular sailing. With nothing to grip the sea, she rolled and pitched alarmingly, throwing both men and supplies around so much that some loose barrels and spare timber had to be thrown over the side for fear of injury.

Nevertheless, the expedition plodded on, picking up a team of dogs at Khabarova, on the north coast of Siberia, and passing Cape Chelyuskin on September 9. *Fram* was the second ship to ever accomplish this. A week later the expedition headed north, following an area of warm currents that created a clear passage through the ice. Nansen's plan was to try and round the New Siberian Islands, but the path was blocked by ice and, after a few more days of traveling deeper into the ice pack, *Fram* came to a stop on September 22. Within a few days they were encased by ice, and both the rudder and the propeller were pulled in to protect them from damage. It would be nearly three years before the ship was fully released from the floe's icy manacles.

The vessel's design principles were soon put to the test as the first wave of ice pressure took hold. There was a "deafening noise," and the ship began to shake as she was slowly lifted several feet out of the water. She was held there for several hours while the ice gnawed at her hull, before she was eventually dropped back into her pool. This happened again and again over the coming weeks, but each time, *Fram* responded just as Nansen had hoped. She simply rose above the ice before she was returned undamaged to the water. After a while Nansen could relax and enjoy the ride, safe in the knowledge that at least one of his tenets had been vindicated.

"It begins with a gentle crack and moan along the side of the ship, which gradually sounds louder in every key," Nansen wrote. "Now a high plaintive tone, now it is a grumble, now it is a snarl, and the ship gives a start up. The noise steadily grows till it is like all the pipes of an organ; the ship trembles and shakes, and rises by fits and starts, or is sometimes gently lifted. There is a pleasant comfortable feeling listening to all this uproar and knowing the strength of our ship."

There were some encouraging signs for his theory that the vessel would drift with the currents toward the North Pole. Despite performing a couple of disconcerting pirouettes, *Fram* was edging forward in a northwesterly direction—although it was painfully slow. Six months after locking into the ice, she had cleared only one degree of latitude, and she had another ten to go. At that rate it would take another five years to reach the North Pole. And their soundings showed that, far from being a shallow area of sea off a plateau of land as previously imagined, the Arctic had large areas of ocean over 12,000 feet (3,657 m) deep. This meant that the

Nansen was a polymath and was easily bored. He studied zoology at a university but was also a proficient sportsman, artist, and then later, a politician.

currents in the region had far less influence than Nansen had anticipated.

After eighteen months stuck in the ice, Nansen couldn't stand it any longer. He decided to leave with one man, his trusted lieutenant, Hjalmar Johansen, and make a dash for the North Pole by sleigh. He knew that it would be impossible to find *Fram* once they had achieved their mission, but he planned to head back south to the island of Spitsbergen, where they would be sure to find a ship to take them back to Norway. *Fram* would continue her journey with the ice in the capable hands of skipper Otto Sverdrup. Where she would end up was anyone's guess.

On March 14, 1895, Nansen and Johansen set off with three sleighs, two kayaks, twenty-eight dogs, and provisions for 100 days. The trip proved much tougher than either man had anticipated, and after three weeks they had covered just 125 miles (200 km)—and they still had 230 miles (370 km) to go. In addition, once they reached the North Pole, they would face another 600 miles (965 km) to return to land. It was unlikely their provisions would last that long at the speed they were going and, besides, as Nansen wrote, "we are undeniably worn out." Therefore, on April 7 Nansen and Johansen hoisted the Norwegian flags at a latitude of 86° 14"—the farthest north anyone had traveled—and turned toward home.

It was to be another sixteen months before they made it to Norway. After an arduous trek across the ice, killing off the dogs one by one to feed the others, they finally arrived at Franz Josef Land—a group of 191 ice-covered islands—just as the Arctic winter arrived. Unable to go any farther, they built a small hut made out of stones and lived there for nine

"It begins with a gentle crack and moan along the side of the ship, which gradually sounds louder in every key. Now a high plaintive tone, now it is a grumble, now it is a snarl, and the ship gives a start up."

months, surviving off walrus, bear, and seal meat. They set off again in May 1896 and a few weeks later bumped into the British explorer Frederick Jackson, who had set up camp at Franz Josef Land two years earlier. Two months later, in August 1896, Nansen

and Johansen sailed into the port of Vardø in northern Norway to the amazement of many people.

Meanwhile, *Fram* continued with her journey across the Arctic Circle. Six months after Nansen had raised the flag at 86° 14" north, she arrived by her own means at 85° 57" north—only 17 miles (27 km) off Nansen's latitude and in considerably greater comfort. But her crew faced another winter in the ice before the ship

started heading south on her own accord. Finally, on August 11, 1896, she broke free just north of Spitsbergen. Her crew heaved a sigh of relief as the engine roared into life and they made their way down a channel toward the open sea. By a strange coincidence they arrived in Norway just a week after Nansen and Johansen, each traveling parallel journeys in wildly different circumstances.

Although Nansen did not achieve his dream of reaching the North Pole, he had gone farther north than anyone else. And perhaps more important, his theory of Arctic drift was proved to be correct, if not quite as swiftly as he had hoped. He had also found

that there was no land on the Siberian side of the Arctic, but just a vast, bottomless ocean. These were all major developments for the science of oceanography, an area that would occupy much of Nansen's future life. It would be twelve years before Robert Edwin Peary made his contentious claim to the North Pole, but by then Nansen was pursuing a diplomatic career, for which he would eventually be awarded a Nobel Peace Prize. The Arctic explorer had left the ice behind him. He turned his attention to the human condition and, it seems, found it slightly less impenetrable.

Fram **was the first polar ship to use "fore-and-aft" sails rather than the traditional "square" sails. She also had a state-of-the-art triple expansion steam engine.**

Gjøa

Overall length
72 ft. (22 m)

Beam
11 ft. (3.4 m)

Draft
3 ft. (1 m)

Displacement
47 tons

Rig
Sloop

Built
Kurt Johannesson Skaale,
Rosendal, Norway

Year
1872

Interesting facts
The first recorded attempt to find the Northwest Passage was in 1539, when Hernán Cortés commissioned Francisco de Ulloa to sail the length of the Baja California Peninsula in search of the so-called Strait of Anián. In 1576–78, Martin Frobisher made three trips to the Canadian Arctic to look for the passage, while in 1609 Henry Hudson ventured up the river that now bears his name to find it. In 1762 the British ship *Octavius* became trapped in ice while looking for it in Alaska. According to legend, she was found thirteen years later in Greenland, with the frozen corpses of her crew still on board, giving her the dubious distinction of being the first ship to cross the passage unaided. The prize for finding the route went to Commander Robert McClure and his crew on HMS Investigator, who crossed from west to east in 1850–54, although part of their journey was completed by sledge.

For 400 years the quest for The Northwest Passage had lured sailors to their doom. Then in 1903 a young man of modest means set out with the smallest expedition ever mounted. But how would the diminutive *Gjøa* survive the rigors of three Arctic winters?

A Magnetic Attraction

Roald Amundsen (1903)

At last! The great adventure for which my whole life had been a preparation was under way! The Northwest Passage—that baffling mystery of the past—was at last to be ours!"

These are the words of Roald Amundsen in his biography *My Life as an Explorer*, and it's hard not to be carried along by his excitement and sense of purpose. As it turns out, his account of the expedition glosses over many uncomfortable facts, but there is no doubting the importance of his achievement or the bravery he and his men showed on Amundsen's very first exploration voyage.

Almost as soon as the Americas were discovered in 1492, there were attempts to find a route to the other side via the north end of the continent. This route would be especially useful for traders who, until the opening of the Panama Canal, had to ship their wares via Cape Horn to reach the West Coast. One of the most famous attempts was made by Sir John Franklin, of the United Kingdom, who journeyed into the ice in 1845 with two ships and 129 men. All of them perished, and for years the mystery of their fate dominated exploration in the area. A huge bounty was offered by the British government to anyone who solved the puzzle, and it is said that more ships and men were lost searching for Franklin and his men than in the original expedition.

One person mesmerized by the Franklin story was young Roald Amundsen. The budding explorer was part of an 1897 Belgian expedition, which became the first team to spend a whole winter in Antarctica. A year later, while stopping off in Grimsby, United Kingdom, Amundsen came across a collection of almost every book written about the Northwest Passage, which he bought and took back with him to Norway. While reading these accounts, he came across a suggestion that the route actually lay much farther south than most expeditions had previously attempted. It would prove to be a crucial piece of information.

It took him three years to find the right boat and arrange the finances, but finally, in June 1903, Amundsen was ready to set off on his own voyage of discovery. His official objective was to find the magnetic north pole, a scientific endeavor for which he was able to raise considerable support. His private mission was to conquer the Northwest Passage. As a relative newcomer to the exploration business, however, his budget was correspondingly modest and could provide for only one 72-foot (22-m) former herring boat with a crew of six men and twenty dogs—a far cry from the mighty expeditions of his hero, Franklin. He would later find himself grateful for only being able to afford such a small craft.

At midnight on June 16, Amundsen and his crew cast *Gjøa* off from the dock of Christiania and headed for the open sea—and not a moment too soon. One of Amundsen's sponsors was already clamoring for his money, and there was a danger that the boat might fall prey to the creditors if they stayed another day. Instead, the ship headed for the west coast of Greenland across the treacherous Melville Bay and into the Northwest Passage proper. They got off to a good start. "As if by an act of God, the ice opened up and we advanced rapidly toward land without any hindrance," Amundsen reported. Soon they were in uncharted water, however, and had to rely on their own soundings to make sure they didn't run aground.

> **"As if by an act of God, the ice opened up and we advanced rapidly toward land without any hindrance."**

Despite their precautions, they hit reefs twice, and they were lucky to float free both times—saved by the ship's comparatively small draft. As if to remind them of the danger of their journey, they found several remains of Franklin's ill-fated expedition as well as the attempted rescue missions that followed.

As the days grew shorter, they found a sheltered cove on King William Island, not far from where the magnetic pole was thought to be located, and set up camp for the winter. Several of the packing cases were designed to be converted into an observatory, complete with a marble floor and nonferrous copper fastenings to house all of the sophisticated instruments that Amundsen had brought. Although it was specifically designed to be nonmagnetic, the hut became known as The Magnet, or Villa Magnet.

The *Gjøa* crew was soon joined by a tribe of Inuit, curious to befriend the first white men they had seen since James Clark Ross, who had arrived seventy-two years before. Amundsen became increasingly fascinated by the tribe and, over the course of the next few months, acquired an enormous collection of Inuit artifacts, which would eventually end up in museums in Norway. His deals were embarrassingly one-sided: two complete sets of women's clothes in return for an empty tin; four white fox skins for the price of a needle. Not only

exhausted but empty-handed. One woman particularly seems to have had several of the men in her thrall, the beautiful Kimaller, of whom Amunsen said: "Her beautiful eyes and profoundly mournful expression made her very attractive. She possessed what I have not found among the fair sex of the Netchjilli Eskimos—grace."

After two years at King William Island, Amundsen and his assistant, Gustav Wiik, still had not conclusively found the magnetic pole. However,

> Two weeks after leaving King William Island, they spotted a sail ahead of them. And there was only one place a ship could have sailed from: the Bering Strait, at the other end of the Northwest Passage. They had made it.

they had collected a huge amount of data about it—enough to keep the scientists busy for the next twenty years, according to Amundsen. On August 13, 1905, the crew broke camp and set sail on the last and most risky part of their voyage: the virgin Simpson Strait, which had never been crossed by ship before. Once again, Amundsen was grateful for *Gjøa*'s minimal draft as they crept along these unknown shallows. At one point it passed with only an inch to spare under the ship's keel.

Two weeks after leaving King William Island, they spotted a sail ahead of them. And there was only one place a ship could have sailed from: the Bering Strait, at the other end of the Northwest Passage. They had made it. For days Amundsen had been unable to eat because of nerves. Now that his life's mission was almost achieved, he grabbed a knife and slashed slice after slice of caribou meat and ate it raw, before becoming sick over the side and starting again. It was a very Nordic celebration.

What happened next is disputed among historians. In his account of the voyage, Amundsen claims that encroaching ice forced them to pull in near King's Point, in northern Canada, and spend

Amundsen had dreamed of becoming a polar explorer from the age of 15, after reading about the exploits of his hero John Franklin.

that, but many of the objects he used to barter with the Inuit were knocked out by the ship's smithy in his forge onboard *Gjøa*. "It was," Amundsen reported with no trace of irony, "a perfect example of a good bargain, in which both sides profited."

Aside from trading with the Inuit and exchanging cultural insights, the Norwegians took more than a passing interest in the Inuit women. Despite Amundsen's assertion that he "took the first opportunity to have a most serious talk with my companions and urge them not to yield to this kind of temptation," there is evidence that his advice was not heeded. Many a so-called "hunting trip" in the ensuing months would end with the men returning

another winter in the ice. Others contend that he wanted to make the voyage look more impressive by staying another year, or perhaps he was trying to stage-manage the news with a dramatic late arrival. Either way, he was certainly eager to let the world know his joyous news. A few weeks after arriving at King's Point, he walked 800 miles (1,300 km) to reach the nearest telegraph station and spent two months selling his story to the newspapers before returning to his ship. Soon after, the ship mourned the loss of its youngest crew member and Amundsen's assistant, Gustav Wiik, who died of a fever—the only person lost during the entire voyage.

Gjøa finally set sail again in June 1906 and crossed the "finish line" between Siberia and Alaska at the end of August. Rather than sail the boat back to Norway, Amundsen donated her to the people of San Francisco for public display. She was returned to Norway in 1972 and has been berthed at the Norwegian Maritime Museum near Oslo ever since. Amundsen's achievement of his boyhood dream ensured that his name would soon be as well known as Franklin, and he would never be short of funding for his voyages again. Before long, he would go on to greater triumphs as he joined the race for the South Pole. The voyage of the little *Gjøa*, however, would always remain close to his heart.

A close relationship developed between the local Inuit tribe and the crew of the *Gjøa*, resulting in trade, cultural exchange, and, it is claimed, romance.

Campina

Overall length
57 ft. (17.5 m)

Beam
15 ft. 3 in. (4.5 m)

Draft
4 ft. (1.2 m) board up
9 ft. (2.7 m) board down

Displacement
28 tons

Sail Area
1,668 sq. ft. (155 m²)

Designer
Caroff, France

Launched
1992

Interesting facts
Henk de Velde has sailed
around the world four times,
three of which were solo and
nonstop. The first lasted from
1978 until 1985. As well as
being an avid aventurer and
sailor, he has written several
books, in all of which he
contemplates the idea of
freedom. Many consider
him to be a philosopher.
He has also directed two
documentaries called *Sea of
Heartbreak* (1997) and *1000
Days of Loneliness* (2005) and
works with the Dutch media.
  "Why do I want to go to
difficult, far-off dangerous
places like Bouvetoya, St
Paul, Cambell of the
Auckland islands, Wrangel
of Tuktoyaktuk? Why? Why
do I not sail right away to the
tropical paradises in the
Pacific Ocean? The reason is:
I am still too much of a child.
The child I was at the age of
ten, when I bought with my
first earned money an atlas…
to dream by. The boy with a
dream to become a ship's
captain and an explorer."

Around the world, east to west, west to east, single-handed, with a crew—you name it—Henk de Velde had done it. So he devised his own challenge: to sail around the world north to south via the Arctic waters of Siberia and around Cape Horn. It was to be a voyage like no other.

The Impossible Voyage

Henk de Velde (2001)

Etta severn, etta lodt." The words rang through Henk de Velde's head as he watched a loose bit of ice floe press *Campina* against the large iceberg to which she was moored. The boat leaned over 10 degrees, and there was a terrible cracking sound. Trapped between two walls of ice, one of them reaching high above water, there was nothing de Velde could do but wait and see if the yacht would be crushed, like so many ships before her, or whether the ice would part again and let her free. Memories of the explorers Barends, Scott, and Shackleton and their fatal missions in the ice filled his thoughts.

After 15 minutes *Campina* popped back up, and de Velde rushed below to see if any water was leaking into the bilge. It was dry. Back on deck, he looked over the side and saw that the propeller and the twin rudders were surrounded by ice. He eased the boat into forward gear, and the propeller slowly cleared the ice away. So far so good, but now he discovered that he had lost steerage. The port rudder was skewed at 60 degrees, while the starboard rudder was not responding at all. The hydraulic system had ruptured and was leaking oil. *Campina* was crippled and, without steerage, would be unable to continue her journey through the ice. Once again, as so often in the Arctic, the elements had asserted their power, and it was pointless to argue. "*Etta severn, etta lodt,*"

the Russians say. "This is the north. This is the ice."

De Velde had started his amazing voyages nearly three decades before when, in 1978, he had set off with his then wife Gini to sail around the world on their homemade catamaran. They had sailed via the Panama Canal into the Pacific, where Gini gave birth to their son Stefan on Easter Island in 1979, and cruised those sun-kissed isles for several years. In 1984, however, the couple separated and de Velde was left to finish the circumnavigation on his own, eventually returning home after traveling a total of 50,000 miles (80,460 km) in seven years. Far from turning him off sailing, his period on his own gave him a new obsession. "From that time on," he says, "I wanted to sail nonstop and solo around the world."

It was easier said than done. It took him several years just to get sponsorship for his first attempt in 1989, but eventually—thanks to an unlikely combination of a sunbed manufacturer and a Scotch whiskey distiller—he set off on his 60-foot (18-m) catamaran, *Alisun J&B*, for the big one. His target was 150 days. But it was not to be; his finishing time of 158 days was well outside the record, and he was forced to stop in New Zealand to make repairs to the boat, thereby automatically ruling himself out of any record.

For his next attempt, in 1992, he managed to persuade his sponsors to build him a brand-new boat,

After getting trapped in ice at the village of Tiksi in northern Siberia, de Velde had to endure a winter of constant winds and freezing temperatures of −76°F (−60°C).

another 60-foot (18-m) catamaran, called the *ZeemanTextielSupers*. The voyage again finished in disaster, however, when the yacht collided with a floating container just three days from the finish and de Velde had to be rescued by a passing Russian freighter. He ended up in a hospital with two fractures to his skull. Was he put off? Not at all. Three years later he was back with a 71-foot (21-m) catamaran, *C1000*. It was a lucky third time for de Velde, because he made it around in 119 days, although by then the record stood at 109 days, so he was still outside it. Instead, he had to be content with being the only person to have sailed a catamaran around the world solo and nonstop.

By now the Flying Dutchman had sailed around the world four times, sailing both from west to east and east to west, and rounded Cape Horn three times. The journeys had consumed twenty years of his life and had gave him enormous satisfaction, but he started to think it was time to do something different—something impossible. And what could be more impossible than sailing around the world from north to south? He couldn't literally sail from pole to pole—at least not without a very large sleigh. But he could do the next best thing, which was to sail around the back of Siberia, through the Northeast Passage, down the Bering Strait, around Cape Horn, and back up the Atlantic. It would be his very own "impossible voyage."

Sailing in the frozen waters north of Siberia was an extremely hazardous voyage undertaken only by a handful of yachts, and he would need something a lot more solid than a high-speed catamaran to cross it.

De Velde and a helper try to clear the ice from the back of the boat—its most vulnerable area. Temperatures rarely rose above –31°F (–35°C).

The solution was *Campina*, a chunky 57-foot (17-m) monohull built of steel and virtually indestructible, although no one had told that to the ice.

Starting off from Holland in 2001, he headed north up the coast to Norway, intending to cut eastward across the top of Russia. He went as far as Murmansk, when he was turned back by bureaucracy: The Russian authorities refused him permission to go any farther. Undaunted, the fearless Dutchman headed north as far as he possibly could, north of the island of Spitsbergen, to latitude 81.20—almost level with the northernmost tip of Greenland—before

most of his loop; now he just needed to get back across to Murmansk to finish his circumnavigation of the world from north to south.

This time luck was with him, and at the small port of Provideniya, near the easternmost tip of Russia, he finally received permission to enter the inner recesses of the Arctic Ocean. Accompanied by an "ice pilot," Boris Volnij, he set off in 2003 and managed to get halfway across before the short Arctic summer ended and the ice closed in on him near the village of Tiksi. Although nuclear-powered ice breakers keep both ends of the Northeast Passage clear for commercial shipping, most of the middle section is seldom used, and it freezes over for most of the year. De Velde therefore had only a two-month weather window to

"Here, world news is not important. Ice governs. Think of the fatal travels of Barends, Scott, and Shackleton. The word 'fail' does not exist in the dictionary of adventurers."

heading south as far as he could, to Cape Horn. His 20,000-mile (32,000-km) voyage took him back up through the Pacific to the Bering Strait and to the other end of the Northeast Passage. He completed

complete his crossing. In the meantime, he had to endure a winter of typical Siberian temperatures, ranging from a relatively balmy –31°F (–35°C) to a wincingly cold –76°F (–60°C).

On August 20, 2004, his break came, and *Campina* sailed west once again. But she didn't get very far. Barely two weeks out of Tiksi, while they were still in the Laptev Sea, the yacht became trapped in ice. "For two days we had laid rather comfortably moored to an ice chunk in 4 feet (3 m) of water," wrote de Velde. "Ice floes clashed against each other constantly with a power enough to crack my ship. Around four hours before darkness fell, the iceberg that we had been anchored to broke. We maneuvered *Campina* to a larger iceberg, between the floating ice. Then the flow twisted and a heavy iceberg pressed the boat against the wall of ice. I heard an enormous cracking."

With the yacht's rudders out of action, de Velde and his pilot had no option but to tie *Campina* to another iceberg while they contemplated their next move. De Velde was eager to repair the damage and continue with his circumnavigation, but he knew that within a few weeks the boat would be encased in ice and he would be stuck in Siberia for another long winter. It was probably the memory of those howling –76°F (–60°C) winds that persuaded him to

make the sensible choice. A Russian freighter as well as an accompanying icebreaker would be passing soon, and de Velde decided to seize the opportunity. At 2:45 A.M., in strong winds and with the ever-present threat of loose ice, *Campina* was craned onto the deck of the *Yuriy Arshenevskiy*, en route to Tiksi. There, while the freighter unloaded its cargo of wood, Boris left the ship and headed back home to the Ukraine. A few weeks later *Campina* unloaded in Murmansk, and de Velde made the necessary repairs before sailing home to the Netherlands, where he arrived in December of that year.

He completed his circumnavigation—albeit with the assistance of a nuclear icebreaker—and he had learned another lesson. "In the north Arctic other laws rule. '*Etta severn, etta lodt*,' say the Russians. 'This is the north. This is the ice.' Here, world news is not important. Ice governs. Think of the fatal travels of Barends, Scott, and Shackleton. The word 'fail' does not exist in the dictionary of adventurers. You set out the challenge and lose or win. If you lose, a next chance comes."

By the age of 52, de Velde had sailed around the world four times, but his final venture marked the first time he sailed in the Arctic.

Pacific

Kon Tiki

Interesting facts

In Inca mythology, Kon Tiki (or Con-Tici Viracocha) was the creator of civilization. One story tells how he destroyed all the people of Lake Titicaca with a Great Flood, saving just two beings who went on to found the Inca civilization.

Friedrich Wilhelm Heinrich Alexander Freiherr von Humboldt (Alexander von Humboldt for short) was a Prussian botanist and explorer. Between the years of 1799–1804 he traveled to South America and explored the Orinoco and Amazon rivers, among other places.

He was also the first to identify the movement of a current off the west coast of South America which was then named after him.

Born in Larvik in 1914, Thor Heyerdahl showed an early interest in zoology and anthropology. His mother was an ardent Darwinist and his father a master brewer. At just eight years old, he started drawing pictures of the South Sea islands and decided he

wanted to be an explorer. He later studied biology and geography at the University of Oslo and organised his first study trip to Polynesia in 1937.

He didn't claim to prove that the current Polynesians came from South America, but that an extinct race, the "short-eared people" mentioned in Polynesian legends could have come from South America by the method he was suggesting

Thor Heyerdahl was determined to prove that the Pacific Islands
had once been visited by the peoples of South America.
So he built a raft of balsa wood and bamboo and set out to sail
4,000 miles (6,400 km) to Polynesia. His voyage ran against the
mass of opinion, from academics to sailors.

In the Wake of the Sun King

Thor Heyerdahl (1947)

The Humboldt current runs northward up the west coast of South America before sweeping out westward across the Pacific. The upcoming cold water, rich in nutrients, creates one of the most fertile marine ecosystems in the world. An entire food chain, from plankton to sardines to sharks and a multitude of birds, thrives in this environment, and around 20 percent of the world's fish that are caught comes from these waters.

The current is also a great transportation route, and for centuries it was used by local inhabitants to travel up the coast on local rafts, or pae-pae, sometimes as far as the Galapagos Islands. Could it also have been used to propel humans even farther afield, perhaps all the way to the Pacific Islands? This was the theory proposed by Norwegian archeologist Thor Heyerdahl. While living off the land on the Marquesa Islands in the 1930s, he realized that many of the plants—such as the sweet potato and the coconut tree—were identical to those found in South America. It occurred to him that some of the imposing stone statues and pyramids found in such places as the Easter Islands also bore a striking similarity to sculptures and buildings created by the Incas of Peru. He was particularly fascinated by the legend of the wise king called Kon-Tiki, or the Sun King, who is said to have fled South America at about

the same time as a similar figure is supposed to have arrived in the Polynesian Islands.

This line of thinking was very much against the conventional wisdom of the time, however, and Heyerdahl's ideas received little recognition from fellow archaeologists. They maintained that the Pacific Islands had been populated by a migration of peoples from the west and that it would have been impossible for primitive people to navigate the Pacific as far as the Easter Islands, approximately 20,000 miles (3,000 km) off the coast of South America, let alone the islands farther west.

But Heyerdahl was not a man that took no for an answer. Determined to prove that his theory was at least possible, if not probable, he decided to build a raft identical to those described by the conquistadores and make the crossing himself. His idea soon gained support from unlikely sponsors. The U.S. military, in the aftermath of World War II, were eager to test a whole range of gadgets and food supplies in extreme conditions—from food rations to antishark powder. The president of Peru, flattered that his country might be the progenitor of a race of people, gave the project free access to a naval base and personnel to help build the raft. And funding wasn't too hard to come by, because many people were willing to give their support to such an adventurous concept.

The best method to catch sharks was to grab them by their tails and drag them on board.

In one day, the *Kon Tiki* crew caught nine sharks, two tuna, and several bonitos.

Heyerdahl's choice of sailing companions was interesting. Even though he proposed sailing across 4,000 miles (6,400 km) of sea, only one of his five crew was a sailor. Knut Haugland and Torstein Raaby were both Norwegian resistance fighters whom Heyerdahl had met during the war; Herman Watzinger was an engineer whom he met in New York; Bengt Danielsson was a Swedish explorer who turned up in Peru a few weeks before the trip and was the only non-Norwegian member of the team; and Erik Hesselberg was an artist and sailor—and the only person on board who knew how to use a sextant.

Like the traditional pae-pae, the raft was built of balsa logs lashed together with rope. Just getting the wood was an adventure. After flying to the Ecuadorian capital, Quito, 9,300 feet (2,800 m) above sea level, Heyerdahl and Watzinger helped cut down the trees and then rode the two rafts of logs

down the Palenque River back to the sea. Next, the timber was transported by ship to Lima. Once cut to size, the central log was 45 feet (14 m) long, with four shorter logs on either side creating an arrow shape. Balsa logs were lashed crossways and overlaid with bamboo to make a deck, and an 8- by 14-foot (2.4- by 4.3-m) bamboo hut was erected to provide some shelter from the elements. Two lengths of sturdy mangrove wood were lashed together in the shape of an upside-down V to make a mast, and a simple rectangular sail hoisted on a bamboo yard completed the rig.

It didn't look like a suitable craft to cross an ocean, and at the last minute the Peruvian Navy,

> **"I knew all the time in my heart that a prehistoric civilization had been spread from Peru and across to the islands at a time when rafts like ours were the only vessel on that coast."**

horrified by the ragged contraption they had helped produce, begged Heyerdahl to cancel the expedition. But he was unrepentant. "I knew all the time in my heart that a prehistoric civilization had been spread from Peru and across to the islands at a time when rafts like ours were the only vessel on that coast," he wrote. "And I drew the general conclusion that, if balsa wood had floated and lashings held for Kon-Tiki in A.D. 500, they would do the same for us now if we blindly made our raft an exact copy of his."

The *Kon-Tiki*, as the raft was christened, was launched on April 27, 1947, and set off from Lima with her crew of six men and one parrot—a last-minute gift—the following day. Heyerdahl and his men had enough provisions on board for four months, a ham radio, and an inflatable dinghy with oars. In front of them lay open sea, mostly a long way from the existing shipping routes. Their raft was unproven, and the voyage ran against the mass of opinion, from academics and sailors alike, who believed that the vessel would either become waterlogged or disintegrate long before it reached land. They also did not have a life raft, survival suits, a satellite radio, and emergency distress beacons—they didn't exist yet. If anything went wrong, they would have to rely on their own resources to get them out of trouble. People thought they were crazy.

Their faith in their unlikely craft was soon put to the test. The very next day, the trade winds sprang up out of the southeast and started pushing them westward. Before long the back of the raft was engulfed by enormous waves, and even with two men on the steering oar, it was a struggle to control the vessel. It took all of their strength to stay on course, and even when their watches were reduced from two hours to one, they were soon exhausted. After sixty hours the raft stalled with her bow pointing into the wind, so the crew furled the sail and left her to ride out the gale. They had already lived through the worse weather that the Pacific would throw at them, and Kon-Tiki had proved herself worthy of their trust. The key to her success was that she flexed her way over the waves, and even the biggest seas simply passed through her open structure "as through the prongs of a fork."

After the trade winds, they made steady progress across the Pacific, always making more than 9 miles (14.5 km) a day and, on one occasion, notching up to an impressive 71 miles (114 km). Their average during the whole crossing was 46.5 miles (75 km) a day.

The richness of the Humboldt current ensured that they never went hungry, either. From the outset they were able to add to their supplies with a rich harvest from the sea. The raft was always surrounded by bonito fish, which they caught with a fishing line, as well as flying fish, squid, tuna, pilot fish, and sharks—though they became so fond of the pilot fish that it was taboo to catch them. They devised a remarkable hands-on method of catching sharks, which consisted of luring the fish near the raft with bait, grabbing its tail as it passed, and then dragging it on board. On one particularly bloody day, they caught nine sharks, two tuna, and several bonito. "To starve to death was impossible," Heyerdahl observed.

Finally, after ninety-three days at sea, they sighted land. It was the island of Pukapuka. By the time they had spotted it, however, the currents had already pushed them too far north and they had to stand by and watch it disappear over the horizon. It was

another three days before they saw land again. This time it was the island of Angatau, but dangerous reefs circled the atoll, and once again they were unable to make landfall. A few days later the currents took matters into their own hands, and Kon-Tiki was driven ashore on Raroia reef, in the Tuamotu Islands, approximately 550 miles (885 km) from Tahiti. After 101 days at sea, Heyerdahl had proved that man could cross the Pacific on a raft.

Although the Kon-Tiki voyage attracted massive media interest and turned Heyerdahl and his beardy crew into celebrities, it failed to impress the majority of archaeologists who regarded his methods as unscientific. The public chose to disagree, and Heyerdahl's book Kon-Tiki: Across the Pacific by Raft was translated into sixty-five languages and sold over 20 million copies. His film of the voyage won the 1951 Oscar for best documentary. He went on to make several other journeys in a variety of ethnic crafts and became an outspoken campaigner for the environment. But for sheer bravery and utter conviction, few voyages could match his original adventure, sailing in the wake of the Sun King.

The Kon Tiki crew was marooned at Raroia for several days before being towed to Tahiti.

Opposite: Heyerdahl climbs the mast of his primitive craft.

Destiny

Overall length
44 ft. 7 in. (13.6 m)

Beam
13 ft. (4 m)

Draft
6 ft. 10 in. (2 m)

Displacement
13 tons

Type
Norseman 447

Interesting facts
The Queen's Birthday Storm has since been compared to the 1979 Fastnet race in the United Kingdom. It didn't claim as many lives, but some say it was an even greater storm due to stronger winds and a greater duration, meaning that the boats were having to survive out at sea for greater lengths of time. The number of people involved in keeping hope

alive ranged from the sailors on the boats, radio operators and volunteers onshore, to the rescuers themselves.

The yachts involved in the storm, later known as the Mayday yachts due to the number of Mayday signals being let off, were:

Heart Light (US): 41 ft. (12.5 m); *Mary T* (US): 40 ft. (12 m); *Pilot* (US): 32 ft. (9.8 m); *Quartermaster* (NZ): 40 ft.

(12 m); *Ramtha* (AUS): 38 ft. (11.5 m); *Silver Shadow* (NZ) 42 ft. (12.8 m); *Sofia* (NZ) 32 ft. (9.8 m); *Waikiwi II* (NZ) 44 ft. (13.4 m)

When Dana and Paula Dinius left Auckland, New Zealand, for the Pacific island of Tonga in June 1994, it was supposed to be a routine crossing to their winter cruising grounds. Five days later they were struggling for survival in one of the worst storms on record.

Dicing with Destiny

Dana and Paula Dinius (1994)

It became known as the Queen's Birthday Storm because it took place over the weekend of Queen Elizabeth II's official birthday in New Zealand. Others referred to it as a meteorological "bomb." Either way, the small area of low pressure that developed north of New Zealand on June 3, 1994, deepened with dramatic intensity and, as it butted against two areas of high pressure to the south, produced winds of 65 to 90 knots and seas of around 35 to 50 feet (10 to 15 m)—some say over 90 feet (27 m). An estimated sixty yachts were in the area, making the autumn pilgrimage from New Zealand to the South Pacific at the end of the cyclone season. By the close of the weekend, seven boats had been abandoned, twenty-one crews had been rescued, and three people had died. And the very last thing anyone was thinking about was the Queen's birthday.

For Dana and Paula Dinius on their yacht, *Destiny*, it was just another routine crossing. The couple had set off from California on their 45-foot (14-m) cruising boat five years earlier and, after sailing by Mexico and the North Pacific, came to New Zealand in 1991. Since then, they used the country as their base to go cruising in the Pacific during the winter months. They had already crossed the 1,000 miles (1,600 km) between New Zealand and Tonga several times and knew the waters well. The pair had had four days of good weather after leaving Auckland, with a friendly breeze pushing them on their way north. Dana noticed the low pressure forming on June 3, however, and as a precaution they effectively stalled the yacht while they worked on her—and prepared her for bad weather. By evening they were surfing down 20-foot (6-m) waves in 30 knots of wind and, despite shortening sail, the boat was going fast—much too fast. Dana decided to set the drogue behind the boat on its long warp and chain, which acted like a brake, and to run under bare poles to try and slow her down. As the wind built up during the night, rising gradually to over 80 knots, the yacht's speed increased again, until she was crashing down 50-foot (15-m) waves at speeds of up to 8 knots. Dana stood at the helm throughout the night, trying desperately to keep Destiny pointing downwind. He knew that if she skewed over sideways in this sea, the next wave would almost certainly capsize her.

As a gray dawn came, they were finally able to see the full enormity of the monster that engaged them in battle. The waves were taller than the yacht's mast, and they resembled mountains trying to engulf them. "It was like being in the Sierras," Dana later remembered. "The breaking crests looked like snow on the peaks. It was incredible."

As the wind started to build again, Paula sent out a Pan Pan message to the Kerikeri radio station at the northernmost tip of New Zealand. The controllers at the station would play a crucial part in the events that followed—not only for *Destiny* but for all of the other boats that would eventually send out emergency calls. The Pan Pan message that Paula sent them was one step down from a full Mayday, and it indicated that *Destiny*'s crew were having difficulties but were not in immediate fear of their lives. That assessment would change all too soon.

On the morning of June 4, despite the severity of the conditions, Dana and Paula were coping with the situation. After more than twenty-four hours at the helm, Dana was tired, but the excitement of guiding their little ship through the wildest ride of their lives was keeping him going. And Paula was constantly on hand to encourage him. But then they hit a wave that felt different from the rest. As the wind knocked the boat flat, she was held suspended in the air for what felt like an eternity, before the bow fell into the trough, flying through 70 feet (20 m) of spume and roaring ocean. As the front of the boat dug deep into the sea, the whole boat tipped over in a terrifying death roll.

> Paula knew that she had to get him down below, but she didn't have the strength to carry him. It took them an hour to maneuver his shattered body down the hatchway into the aft bunk.

Dana and Paula were dragged under the water and, when they reemerged, found themselves trapped by broken debris. The mast broke and wrapped itself around the boat's hull. Worse still, Dana was badly injured and could hardly move because of the pain in his leg. After his heroic work at the helm for the past day or so, there was now nothing he could do to help Paula get them out of this mess. The priority was to get rid of the mast, which was crashing against the side of the hull and threatening to punch a hole in it. But the motion of the boat was so violent that, even crawling on all fours, Paula could barely keep herself on deck, much less saw through the wire rigging that was strapping the mast down. Instead, she decided to

get Dana out of the elements. By now his face was ashen and he was trembling with shock. Paula knew that she had to get him down below, but she didn't have the strength to carry him. It took them an hour to maneuver his shattered body down the hatchway and into the aft bunk.

Although Paula had already set off the yacht's Emergency Position Indicating Radio Beacon (EPIRB), there was no way of knowing whether the signal had been received or whether a rescue ship was on its way. And, with the aerial on the mast now under water, the long-range radio was useless. There was nothing to do but wait as *Destiny* was tossed around by the sea. Every now and then, an especially large wave would pitch the boat on her side, throwing her contents—including Dana and Paula—from one side to the other. And the whole time, the mast continued to punch the hull.

Three hours after the capsize, the VHF radio suddenly erupted into life.

"*Destiny*, *Destiny*. This is Kiwi Three One Five. Do you copy? Over."

It was a Royal New Zealand Air Force airplane, sent out from Auckland to search for *Destiny*. Paula was euphoric. Rescue was here! As she spoke to the officers in the plane and discussed Dana's condition with a doctor, she gradually realized that there would be no easy fixes. All the Orion plane could do was track their position and guide a ship toward them. If worse came to worse, they could drop a life raft to them—which was just as well because Paula had discovered that the yacht's life raft, which had self-inflated after the capsize, had torn free.

The closest possible rescue vessel was the 7,246-ton container ship *Tui Cakau*. She was only 30 miles (50 km) away, but she was also struggling with 55-knot winds and 40- to 50-foot (12- to 15-m) waves. It would be hours before she arrived. Meanwhile, the mast had chipped through the hard gel coat on the outside of the hull, and Paula and Dana could hear it shredding the softer layer of fiberglass on the inside. It sounded like an animal, slowly but determinedly burrowing its way into the boat's fragile shell. They knew that once the mast broke through, water would come exploding into the yacht and sink her in minutes.

It was a long night for both the terrified couple on board *Destiny* and the Orion crews that took turns shadowing the yacht. It was also a long night for Captain Jim Hebden on the *Tui Cakau* as he contemplated the rescue ahead. Bringing a 7,000-ton container ship alongside a 45-foot (14-m) yacht in the middle of a hurricane was not going to be an easy job, yet two people's lives depended on his success. The smallest misjudgment could end up with the ship simply mowing the yacht down.

In the early hours of June 5, the *Tui Cakau* arrived after being led to the exact spot by a trail of flares dropped by the RNZAF plane. The ship stood by until dawn and then began its first pass. Captain Hebden's plan was to lower two men down on a life raft onto *Destiny*'s deck and then scoop up the people on board before the yacht was smashed to pieces against the ship's hull. But as he approached with the wind from behind, he realized the ship was going too fast and pulled out of the maneuver. *Tui Cakau* gave the yacht a glancing blow and then lined up for a second pass, this time heading into the wind.

On board *Destiny*, Paula was still recovering from the first, unsuccessful attempt, when the four-story-high hull loomed over them once again. This time a line shot down toward her, and as she tied it to a winch, the yacht was thrown against the steel wall with a crash. A ladder and a life raft floated down the ship's side, and two of the ship's Fijian crew jumped out and threw her into it. As the raft flew back up to deck level, the men went down below where Dana was struggling to get on deck, and they quickly lashed him to a stretcher. The next thing Dana knew, he was being lifted up into the air, thudding against the ship's side as she rolled with the swell. As the two crew clambered up the ladder to safety, Dana was lowered onto the ship's deck. Suddenly, after all those hours of waiting, the Dinius' ordeal was over, and it had all happened in a matter of seconds. With one last, painful thud *Destiny* was cut loose, and the container ship steamed ahead, leaving behind the couple's treasured home of five years.

Elsewhere in the Pacific Ocean seven other boats were also in trouble. In fact, there were so many EPIRBS going off at one point that some yachts were

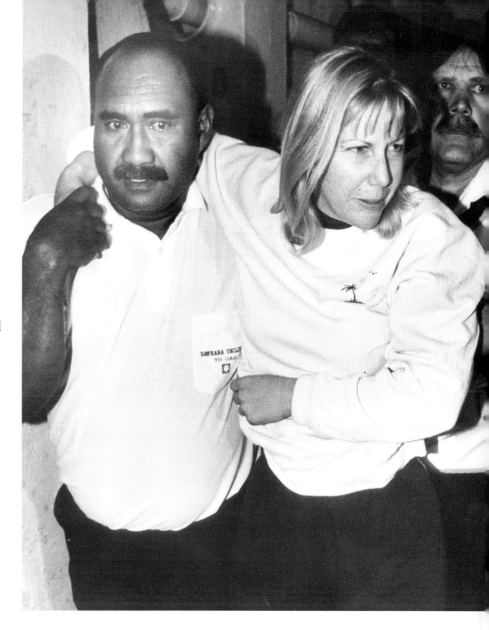

asked to switch theirs off so the rescue planes could distinguish one boat from the other. Eventually, five other crews were lifted to safety by other ships in the area, while another boat made it to the harbor on its own. The three-man crew of the last yacht weren't so lucky, and all that was found of them or their boat was an empty life raft.

Surprisingly, considering their experiences in the Queen's Birthday Storm, Dana and Paula were not completely put off sailing. After going back to California for surgery on Dana's shattered thigh bone, they began discussing the possibilities if they went to sea again. Meanwhile, their valiant yacht continued on its journey alone, eventually washing up on the Banks Islands, north of New Caledonia. It was exactly as destiny intended.

Paula Dinius after being rescued from the Pacific. Overall, twenty-one people were rescued from the storm. Sadly, three sailors didn't make it back to safety.

VC Offshore Stand Aside

Overall length
41 ft. (12.5 m)

Year built
1990

Designer
Jim Young

Interesting facts
The Sydney-to-Hobart race is one of the most popular sporting events in Australia, along with the Davis Cup tennis and Melbourne Cup horse race. It attracts huge media coverage, similar to the Volvo Ocean, America's Cup and Velux 5 Ocean races.

It is open to anyone who owns a yacht that meets safety regulations and is highly popular—many

sailors and yachts come back year after year. The sailors who have competed in the most races are the late John Benetto and Lou Abrahams, who both competed in forty-four races.

The Sydney-to-Hobart was started in 1945 by the British yacht designer John Illingworth. He won the first race on his wooden cutter Rani with a time of 6 days, 14 hours, and 22 minutes. Since

then, the time has steadily been reduced, until even the two-day barrier was broken, by *Nokia* in 1999, with a time of 1 day, 19 hours, and 48 minutes. The slowest-ever race was in 1945, when Peter Luke and his yacht *Wayfarer* took 11 days, 6 hours, and 20 minutes to complete the course. Luke does have the comfort of knowing that his record is never likely to be broken.

The Sydney-to-Hobart race is known as one of the most challenging yachting events in the world. Yet nothing quite topped the 1998 edition: Sixty-six participants retired, five boats sank, fifty-seven people had to be plucked from the sea, and six people lost their lives. From then on, Australian sailing would never be the same.

Hell on Highwater

James Hallion (1998)

There was an undeniable thrill of excitement among the crew of *VC Offshore Stand Aside* as the yacht ran down the east coast of Australia on the evening of December 26, 1998. The wind was coming from behind, and they had both a full mainsail and the spinnaker set—their maximum possible sail area, in other words. These were ideal conditions for the boat's wide lightweight hull, and she surfed down the waves, throwing up spectacular clouds of spray and hitting speeds of up to 18 knots. Every now and then the sails fluttered, then filled again with a sharp crack, as if to remind them of the massive forces at play. This was yacht racing at its exhilarating best, and none of the crew would have wanted to be anywhere else.

The 41-foot (12.5-m) yacht and her crew of twelve were taking part in the Sydney-to-Hobart race, a 630-mile (1,014-km) roller-coaster ride across the Tasman Sea, which is rated as one of the toughest sailing events in the world. The 116-strong fleet set out from Sydney on Boxing Day comprising massive vessels such as the *Sayonara*, owned by the Silicon Valley mogul Larry Ellison, to local family-owned yachts, to the 52-foot (16-m) *Winston Churchill*, a restored wooden veteran of the first Sydney-to-Hobart race, in 1945. Most were hoping to reach Hobart in less than three days, but no one had yet managed to break the two-day barrier. The general idea was for the boats to

arrive in the harbor in time for New Year's Eve, when they would all have an almighty party, Australian style, before cruising gently home in the new year.

As the wind increased to around 30 to 35 knots, skipper and owner James Hallion and his crew set a smaller spinnaker and put a couple of reefs in the mainsail. As dawn came, they were down to a small foresail and triple-reefed main. By then they had passed Eden, on the southeast tip of Australia, their last port of refuge before heading into the notorious Bass Strait. Even in summer the 130-mile (210-km) stretch of water between Australia and Tasmania is well known for whipping up a particularly lethal mix of steep seas and sharp squalls, a combination that is arduous for even the most seasoned boats and sailors. With the wind building from behind, the *Stand Aside* crew knew that once they had passed Eden, they were committed to sailing all the way to Hobart and it would become increasingly difficult to turn back. As it turned out, their roller-coaster ride had just begun.

There was a short lull in the wind during the morning of the twenty-seventh, and Hallion was just beginning to think they might be under-canvassed, when the front finally arrived, belting through the Bass Strait like only a Southern Ocean screamer can do. Within minutes the wind climbed from 55 knots to 60, then 70, and then, incredibly, to 80 knots.

Hallion called all the crew on deck, and they immediately doused both sails—dropped them quickly—and lashed the boom down to prevent it from causing any damage to the boat—or the crew.

Stand Aside was now in extreme conditions, and racing took second place to simply just trying to survive.

> **"The storm intensity probably won't last, we thought, and going back was riskier than keeping going in the direction we were heading."**

Everyone has their own theory about how to handle a boat in such situations, and there were some on board who felt they should sail back to Eden, even though the port was by now approximately ten or twelve hours away and would mean a journey that headed straight into the wind. At least that would keep the boat's nose pointing into the weather rather than to expose her more vulnerable stern. Hallion, however, decided to keep going toward Tasmania—as did most of the fleet caught in the storm that day—and set a small storm jib to maintain steerage. Downwind was, after all, the yacht's strongest point of sail.

"Frankly, the boat was handling the conditions extremely well," he later said, "and we thought, This way, we'll get off the shelf into deeper water

[where the waves are usually less steep]. The storm intensity probably won't last, we thought, and going back was riskier than keeping going in the direction we were heading."

Two hours later waves up to 80 feet (24 m) high were crashing through the Bass Strait. Eight members of *Stand Aside*'s crew were on deck trying to control the boat, while another four were below, two of whom were squeezed into the navigation area about to give their position to race control on the yacht's radio. Suddenly there was a shout from the wave lookout, and a huge wave broke over the stern of the yacht. As the wave broke, it lifted the stern and *Stand Aside* confronted the wave, pummeling into the bottom of it. There was a massive bang as the mast shattered and the boom was smashed into the top of

the cabin. Then the boat rolled over and lay upside down in the water, pinning some of the crew under it while others were dumped into the sea.

"I was tethered to the boat, and the thought crossed my mind, Do I unclip? Is the boat going to come up?" Hallion remembered. "And I thought, No, I've got plenty of air in my lungs, wait. So I knew it wasn't very long at all, no more than thirty seconds. The boat re-righted with quite a lot of force. It was a bit like being tugged by a ski boat. I just went straight back up to the surface."

The scene that greeted him was something out of his worse nightmares. *Stand Aside* was dismasted, with a massive hole in her deck. Most of the crew was in the water, being dragged along by their lifelines, as the yacht slewed down the waves, dragged to one side by

Even the larger yachts, such as the 76-foot (23-m) *Nokia*, struggled under the extreme conditions of the 1998 Sydney-to-Hobart race. The following year, *Nokia* broke the two-hour barrier, setting a new course record of 1 day, 19 hours, 48 minutes.

One of the crew immediately set off the yacht's Emergency Position Indicating Radio Beacon (EPIRB) to alert the Coast Guard that they were in trouble, while another sent out a Mayday on a handheld VHF—the more powerful fixed radios had been drenched during the capsize. Meanwhile, the rest of the crew set about launching the life rafts and cutting the rigging to release the mast to prevent it from punching a hole in the hull. *Stand Aside* carried two six-man life rafts, but as they struggled to launch them, only one inflated. The other stubbornly refused to open and, when the crew tried to retrieve it to pump it up manually, the tether broke and it drifted off to sea. They were now left with one six-man life raft for twelve people in massive waves that appeared more like a snow-covered mountain.

Not only that, but several of the men were injured: One had lost half a finger, another had an injured ankle, and others had varying degrees of cuts and bruises. Registered nurse Andy Marriette patched them up as best he could, and then it was just a matter of waiting until help reached them. Like most sailors the world over, they had all heard about the disastrous 1979 Fastnet race in the United Kingdom and had taken on board the major lesson learned then: Always stay on your boat as long as possible before submitting to a life raft. So the twelve of them huddled together in the cockpit, taking turns to bail out the interior, while the yacht was thrown from wave to wave.

It wasn't long before an Australian Broadcasting Corporation helicopter, sent out to cover the race for that day's news bulletins, picked up their Mayday. With no rescue equipment, however, all they could do was hover in the air above and watch—and take photos—until the rescue services arrived at the scene.

Meanwhile, the 38-foot (11.5-m) *Sienna* had also picked up *Stand Aside*'s Mayday and, despite making good progress in the atrocious conditions, abandoned the race to go to her assistance. Once they reached the stricken yacht, they realized it would be too dangerous for them to attempt a rescue.

Nevertheless, they stayed nearby, sailing up and down for nearly two hours in case *Stand Aside* broke up and its crew had to be pulled from the water. *Sienna* was eventually forced to abandoned its vigil and head for land after it suffered its own knockdown, which left one of its crew with three broken ribs and a punctured lung.

Above: The crew of *Stand Aside* huddle together in the cockpit as their boat starts to break up.

Opposite: A rescued skipper recovers after being airlifted to safety.

the weight of the broken mast. The four men that had been down below when she capsized had come on deck and were helping their crewmates back on board. Belowdecks there was a foot of water sloshing about above the cabin sole, and bits of cabin, food, and clothing were floating everywhere. Most of the internal framework had been torn out, so the boat was twisting alarmingly. It was clear she would probably sink soon.

being lowered on the line, found himself shooting back up in the air several times that day before he could reach the crew members. This later earned him the title Human Teabag.

Once the Helimed team had successfully picked up eight men, they handed the duty over to another helicopter that had arrived on the scene. With four men

> **❝All my values in life have changed. My relationship with my wife is ten times better.❞**

to go, it now became the job of two women—Kristy McAlister and Michelle Blewitt, who were both on their first flying mission—to become the live bait.

On their third lift the raft line became entangled with the hoist wire and had to be cut free, leaving the raft to bounce away over the waves. So, for the final rescue, the last man on board *Stand Aside* had to jump into the water and hang on to a rope, until Blewitt was able to pluck him out of the sea—a brave act in a violent Force 11 storm, with wind speeds of up to 63 knots.

Elsewhere, there were other scenes of devastation. By the end of the race, sixty-six boats had retreated and five had sunk, while fifty-five people had to be rescued and six people lost their lives. It was the worst death toll in the fifty-four-year history of the race.

Yet, for those who survived, there were positive lessons to be learned. Mike Marshman, the crew member who had lost part of his finger on board Stand Aside, told Australian journalist Rob Mundle after the race: "I've been a pretty selfish bastard—just ask my wife. But all the emotions I faced out there really stunned me. All my values in life have changed. My relationship with my wife is ten times better. The house is fun again. I want to spend more time with my kids, and I'm back to actually enjoying my work."

The race organizers had learned a bitter lesson, too, and the entry requirements were considerably tightened thereafter. The race, however, would always retain its nickname Hell on Highwater. After 1998 it had never seemed more apt.

An hour and a half after *Stand Aside* capsized, a helicopter appeared out of the clouds. It was a Helimed. Over the VHF radio the pilot instructed the *Stand Aside* crew to put two men in the life raft and allow the raft to drift astern on a long line. One of the rescue crew was then lowered into the sea; he swam over to the raft and strapped one of the men into a harness. A signal was given, and they were both hoisted back up. Once both men were inside the Helimed, the raft was sent back to the boat to collect the next pair. With the helicopter hovering over 50-foot (15-m) waves, it was impossible to maintain constant height, and Peter Davidson, the rescuer

Kathena Nui

Overall length
35 ft. (10.6 m)

Waterline length
28 ft. (8.6 m)

Beam
10 ft. 10 in. (3.2 m)

Draft
4 ft. 4 in. (1.7 m)

Displacement
5.4 tons

Builder
Uwe Dübbel, Germany

Year
1984

Interesting facts
Chay Blyth was the first person to sail around the world single-handed non-stop the 'wrong' way. He completed his loop in 1971 in 292 days, a record which stood for twenty-three years.

Blyth's record was finally broken by British ocean sailor Mike Golding in 1994, who blistered around in just 161 days. He is the first sailor to have sailed solo around the world in both directions.

The fastest 'westabout' circumnavigation was completed by Frenchman Jean Luc van den Heede on his aluminium monohull *Adrien* in 2004 in 122 days 14 hours and 4 minutes.

Wilfried Erdmann's feat is one of a fairly small number of German sailing achievements. Hans Howaldt won a bronze medal in the 1936 Olympic Games in the 8 Meter class and Peter Bischoff won gold in the Star class.

When Wilfried Erdmann set off on his fifth circumnavigation, he was hardly a youthful man. But the German single-hander found that age was the least of his problems. During his voyage the sailor was to battle weeks of full-force winds, a broken rib, and a dwindling food supply.

Around the World at 60

Wilfried Erdmann (2000)

Go on board a typical Open 60 yacht set up for solo racing and you'll find that much of the boat is scarcely used. Most single-handers rely on one multipurpose living area in the middle of the boat, where they navigate, write, cook, eat, and sleep, often for months at a time. When they're not on deck changing sails or making repairs, they spend most of their time in this relatively small section of the yacht. This leaves the rest of the boat free for sails, food stores, spare parts, and if they're literary types, books.

Pity Wilfried Erdmann, then. When he set off to sail around the world in August 2000, he had to fit nearly a year's worth of stores in just 34 feet (10 m) of boat—that's around half the length of an Open 60 and probably a quarter the volume. Not only that, but his boat was divided into three self-contained watertight compartments, with the living area in the middle. So if he forgot his matches, it wasn't just a matter of popping down to the corner shop; he had to go on deck and forage in one of the storage compartments—all very well in fine weather, but decidedly tricky when the deck is being pressure-hosed by the full might of the Southern Ocean. Nevertheless, he managed to pack in quite a lot of food, including 176 lb. (80 kg) of onions and potatoes grown by his wife, Astrid, in their own garden.

But Erdmann knew what he was doing. Way back in 1966–68 he had sailed single-handedly around the world in a tiny, 24-foot (7-m) wooden boat from Scarborough, United Kingdom, becoming the first German to do so. A year later he was back, this time with his wife, enjoying another leisurely three-year circumnavigation on a slightly larger, 29-foot (9-m) steel yacht. Then, in 1984, he decided to follow the example set by Robin Knox-Johnston on board Suhaili and sail around the world single-handed and nonstop—the ultimate solo challenge. Except that, like Knox-Johnston, he had a limited budget, and 34 feet (10 m) was the longest boat he could afford. Undaunted, he had the aluminum *Kathena Nui* built to an extra-high spec and managed to complete his fourth loop in 271 days, becoming the first German to conquer this amazing task.

Erdmann loved these long voyages. He loved the planning, the logistics, working out how to fit all the stores into such a small space. Everything mattered—if you forgot the simplest thing, such as the paraffin stove nozzle cleaner, then you wouldn't be able to cook for the next nine months. He was proud that the only item that he had left behind on his last circumnavigation had been his hot-water bottle—which was a bad enough omission when you're sailing in near-freezing temperatures. He longed for another

Erdmann's son Kym took this photo as he flew to New Zealand to rendezvous with his father and provide Erdmann with extra supplies as he sailed past the halfway-round-the-world mark.

voyage—this time around the world nonstop the "wrong" way, from east to west, against the prevailing winds and currents.

His wife begged him not to go. He had already been around solo nonstop once, so why do it again? It was fifteen years before she relented. But by then he was 60: a ripe old age to be sweating ropes in the middle of an ocean gale. Suddenly the question was, Is it too late? However, in the end it wasn't Erdmann's age but the size of his boat that was the issue.

All seemed to be going well for the first few weeks as he sped down the Atlantic, but as he turned the corner at Cape Horn and faced the full might of the Southern Ocean, he realized why this was called going the "wrong" way. Whereas on his previous trip the main challenge had been just squeezing everything into the vessel, this time he found that the size of the boat just didn't fit the size of the seas. Faced with relentless gales, *Kathena Nui* simply didn't have the power or the momentum to carry him over the waves. Again and again he was pushed back and found himself actually losing ground to the elements. Even when the wind did subside, the yacht was unable to make headway against the huge swells, and he often had to wait several days before sailing again. On December 17 Erdmann reported that he had only had twenty-two hours' sailing in the right direction in the previous two weeks and had been pushed back 65 miles (104 km) in one day. On one day, December 6, he realized that he was in exactly the same place he had been nearly a week before. Meanwhile, he was being forced farther north, into the Pacific Ocean.

To make matters worse, during the first cluster of gales, the yacht's violent motion threw Erdmann against a winch and broke one of his ribs. For the next few weeks every movement was agony. He took lots of painkillers and rested as much as he could, but with 30- to 40-knot winds blowing outside, the yacht needed constant attention to make sure it wouldn't be blown back to Cape Horn. For two weeks he crawled around the boat on his hands and knees, struggling to do even the simplest jobs. "I couldn't even laugh, it hurt so much," he later said. "But there wasn't much to laugh about anyway."

Erdmann was also concerned about his food supply. When he had provisioned the boat back in Cuxhaven, he had been working on the basis that the voyage would take him around 310 days. But now not only was he going to be at sea for longer than he'd planned, the extra work needed to sail the boat in these conditions was taking its toll and he needed more food to keep going. It was also colder than last time. However, he knew he would have to cut back on his rations rather than eat any more. A slow, gnawing hunger set in, which would stay with him for most of the voyage. More frustrating still, although he could see food around him in the shape of the countless fish that followed the boat, he couldn't touch any of it. Germany's most traveled sailor was allergic to fish.

In the middle of January, *Kathena Nui* hit the worse weather of the trip: five gales in the space of nine days. One knocked the boat back 58 miles (93 km), another 117 miles (188 km). "There is barely a gap between the storms. The swell is absolutely confused, and the sea explodes on the boat like a bomb. If I had a weak heart, I would have collapsed with fright by now," Erdmann reported in his on-line diary. "For over a month I have no favorable wind direction. My oceanic logic slowly crumbles. After the third storm, I had my first serious depression. I haven't been this low since leaving Cuxhaven."

Thankfully, that was to prove the low point of the voyage. Two weeks later *Kathena Nui* emerged out of the Pacific and rounded the southernmost tip of New Zealand. It was a symbolic moment not only because Erdmann could finally stow his heavily marked Pacific chart, but he also had his first face-to-face human contact of the journey. And what an encounter it was. His son Kym had flown out to New Zealand and chartered a plane to fly out and "buzz" his father as he passed land for the first time since Cape Horn. As Kym swooped down close to

the yacht, he dropped a plastic container with an early birthday present for his father. It contained everything the single-hander could desire after six months at sea: some apples, a pack of biscuits, a loaf of bread, a newspaper, and a comb. It was a deeply emotional moment for both men, and Erdmann would later remember the visit as the highlight of his trip.

Three months later marked another high point: rounding the Cape of Good Hope and finally heading north up the Atlantic, out of the eternally combative South Ocean. He could now relax a little and start eating normally, knowing that he would be home in a few weeks. For the first time in over six months, he didn't have constant pangs of hunger.

On July 23, 2001, *Kathena Nui* reached the harbor in Cuxhaven. By then Erdmann had only one box of food left, containing all the food he liked least—mainly anything containing baked beans—and he had lost 22 lb. (10 kg). Two days later and he would have been forced to choose between baked beans and fish. At 343 days, it was one of the slowest circumnavigations on record—partly because he had started from Germany and had to negotiate the English Channel before reaching the Atlantic—but it was the first nonstop east-to-west voyage by a German. And, at 61, Erdmann was only the second person to have complete nonstop circumnavigations in both directions. The happiest person that day, however, was his wife. "It was a moment in life which you cannot have if you live in the normal way," she said. "It was unforgettable."

His wife begged him not to go. He had already been around solo nonstop once, so why do it again?

Bibliography

ATLANTIC OCEAN

Howard Blackburn
Challenge—Lone Sailors of the Atlantic by Gérald Asaria, Sidgwick & Jackson 1979
Les Grands Navigateurs en Solitaire by Benjamin Lambert Bordas 1989

Joshua Slocum
Sailing Alone Around the World by Cpt. Joshua Slocum Adlard Coles Nautical 1996
Voyage of the Liberdade by Cpt. Joshua Slocum Dover 1998

Alain Bombard
The Bombard Story by Alain Bombard
Andre Deutsch 1953
Challenge—Lone Sailors of the Atlantic by Gérald Asaria, Sidgwick & Jackson 1979
Les Grands Navigateurs en Solitaire by Benjamin Lambert Bordas 1989

Donald Crowhurst
The Strange Voyage of Donald Crowhurst by Nicholas Tomalin
Hodder & Stroughton 1970

Fastnet
Fasnet, The Deadliest Storm in the History of Modern Sailing by John Rousmaniere
WW Norton 2000

Knox-Johnston & Blake
Beyond Jules Verne by Robin Knox-Johnston
Hodder & Stoughton 1995

Dom Mee
Personal interview
www.dommee.co.uk

movistar
Personal interview
www.volvooceanrace.org

INDIAN OCEAN

Abernethy & Noel-Smith
Personal interview
www.transventure.com

Michael Briant
Personal interview
www.michaelbriant.com

Raphaëla le Gouvello
Personal interview
www.raphaela-legouvello.com

SOUTHERN OCEAN

Ernest Shackleton
South by Ernest Shackleton
Penguin 1999

Vito Dumas
Alone Through the Roaring Forties by Vito Dumas
International Marine / McGraw Hill 2001
Seuls Autour du Monde by Benoît Heimermann
Éditions Ouest-France 2000

Bernard Moitessier
Tamata and the Alliance by Bernard Moitessier
Waterline 1995
The Long Way by Bernard Moitessier
Sheridan House 1995

Jon Sanders
Lone Sailor by Jon Sanders
St. George Books 1983
Seuls Autour du Monde by Benoît Heimermann
Éditions Ouest-France 2000

Bertrand de Broc
Vendée Globe—Le Grand Souffle by Jean-Yves Montagu
Albin Michel 1993

Pete Goss
Close to the Wind by Pete Goss
Headline 1998
Godforsaken Sea by Derek Lundy
Yellow Jersey Press 2000

Tony Bullimore
Saved by Tony Bullimore
Warner Books 1997
Godforsaken Sea by Derek Lundy
Yellow Jersey Press 2000

Tracy Edwards
Living Every Second by Tracy Edwards,
Coronet 2001

Dee Caffari
Personal interview
www.deecaffari.com

Golding & Thomson
Personal interviews
www.mikegolding.com
www.alexthomsonracing.com

Maud Fontenoy
Personal interview
www.maudfontenoy.com

ARCTIC OCEAN

Fridtjof Nansen
Farthest North by Fridtjof Nansen pub Birlinn 2002
Nansen—The Explorer as Hero by Roland Huntford,
Abacus 2001

Roald Amundsen
My Life as an Explorer by Roald Amundsen,
William Heinemann 1927
Roald Amundsen by Tor Bomann-Larsen,
Sutton Publishing 2006

Henk de Velde
Personal interview
www.henkdevelde.org

PACIFIC OCEAN

Kon Tiki
Kon-Tiki—Across the Pacific by Raft by Thor Heyerdahl
Rand McNally & Co. 1950

Dana & Paula Dinius
Rescue in the Pacific by Tony Farrington
International Marine / Ragged Mountain Press 1998

Sydney-Hobart
Fatal Storm by Rob Mundle
Adalard Coles Nautical 1999
The Proving Ground by G Bruce Knecht
Little, Brown & Co 2001

Wilfried Erdmann
Personal interview
ww.wilfried-erdmann.de

Index

Acknowledgments

Writing this book has been a humbling experience. Whether it was reading some of the greatest maritime literature ever published, or talking to the people who have been out there and experienced extraordinary things first hand, I've been impressed and often awed by the courage and integrity I've come across. In particular I would like to thank Alex Thomson, Mike Golding, Dom Mee, Maud Fontenoy, Wilfried and Astrid Erdmann, Henk de Velde, Barry Pickthall, and Emma Brenton. I would also like to thank Fiona Kellagher at Cassell, who did an excellent job of knocking my words into shape and smoothing the way, Laura Price for getting the whole thing going, and Jennifer Veall for her hard word tracking down seemingly untrackable pictures.

This book is dedicated to my brother Spencer, for being a rock in a storm.

Cassell Illustrated would also like to thank Pete Goss, Mike Noel-Smith, and Michael Briant for their help in supplying informatio and images for the book.

Photo Credits

Alamy/Reinhard Dirscherl 67; /Mike Goldwater 62; /Frank Hurley/Royal Geographical Society 80; /David Trevor 12; /Worldspec/NASA 66

Bluegreen Pictures/Onne van der Wal 87

Michael Briant 64, 65 bottom left, 65 right

Bridgeman Art Library/Museum of Fine Arts, Boston/Otis Norcross Fund/Winslow Homer, The Fog Warning, 1885, 16

Camera Press/N.A./Gamma 90, 93

Cape Ann Historical Association 14

Corbis UK Ltd 78 inset; /C. L. Andrews 156; /Bettmann 18; /Nic Bothma /epa 2; /Dominique Charnay/Sygma 88, 90, 92; /Richard Cummins 36; /Robert Garvey 99; /Goodshoot 164' /Dallas and John Heaton 60; /E. H. Hewitt 154; /Guy Motil 76; /Della Zuana Pascal/Sygma 46 top right; /Mathew Polak 125; /Molly Riley/Reuters 56; /Paul A. Souders 152;

DPPI Agence De Presse/Ajax News 96; /Bertrand de Broc 102, 105; /Pete Goss 106, 110 top right, 110 bottom; /Benoit Stichelbaut 7; /Henri Thibault 46 bottom, 111; /Jacques Vapillon 4, 100, 115

Getty Images 39, 81, 146, 148, 149, 166, 170; /AFP 27 top left, 27 bottom right; /Richard Bouhet/AFP 72, 75, 138, 140, 142, 143; /Gary Cralle 144; /Bill Curtsinger 10; /Julian Herbert 120, 122; /Charles Hewitt 26; /joSon 22; /Mansell/Time & Life Pictures 78, 150; /Marty Melville 59; /Stephen Munday 47; /Adam Pretty 176; /Edmond Terakopian/AFP 129; /William West/AFP 54

www.raphaela-legouvello.com/Jean Marie Liot 74

Henk de Velde 160, 163

Kon Tiki Museum 168, 168, 171

McAllen Library Texas 23

Dom Mee/Barry Roach Murka 50; /Tony Matthews 53

Museum of Yachting 15, 84, 86, 94

New Zealand Herald 175

Mike Noel-Smith 68, 70, 71

onEdition ©2006 6, 9, 126, 128, 130, 132, 133, 137 bottom; /Mike Golding MGYR 137 top

PA Photos 124; /Alfredo Aldai/AP 134; /AP 28; /Barry Batchelor 48, 51; /Joe Gibbons/AP 52; /Martyn Hayhow 121; /Chris Ison 136; /Jon Nash/ABN Amro 58; /Rick Tomlinson 118

PPL Ltd. 30, 32, 34, 35, 98; /D. H. Clarke 20, 21; /Ian Mainsbridge 178, 179, 180; /Tony McDonough/Sportshoot 108, 109 right; /News LTD. 181; /Mark Pepper 1, 42, 44; /RAAF 108 left; /Royal Navy 38, 40, 41; /Henk de Velde 158, 160, 162; /West Australian 112, 116, 117

L. Robbins Collection (original copyright unknown) 172

Royal Geographical Society/Frank Hurley 82, 83; /Roald Amundsen 157

TopFoto/Roger-Viollet 24, 29

Wilfried Erdmann 182, 184, 185

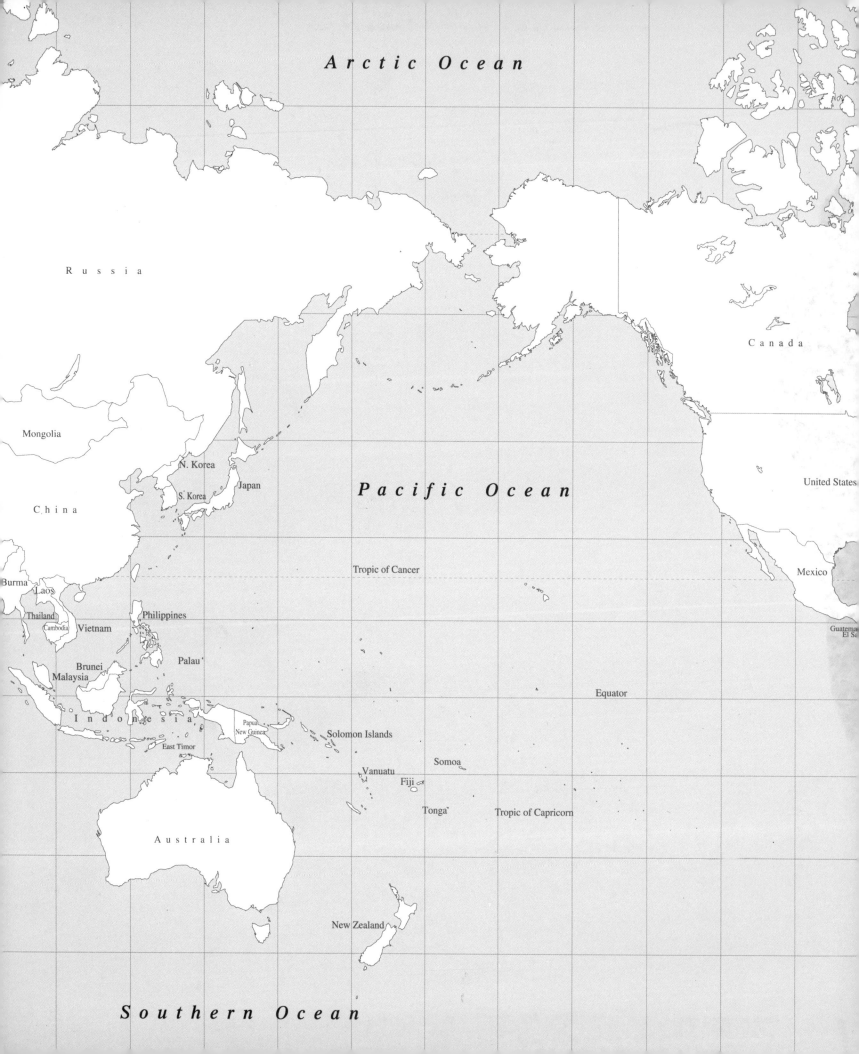

Arctic Ocean

Russia

Canada

Mongolia

N. Korea

Japan

S. Korea

China

Pacific Ocean

United States

Burma   Laos

Thailand

Cambodia   Vietnam

Philippines

Tropic of Cancer

Mexico

Guatema

El Sa

Brunei

Malaysia

Palau

I n d o n e s i a

Papua
New Guinea

Solomon Islands

Equator

East Timor

Vanuatu

Somoa

Fiji

Tonga

Tropic of Capricorn

Australia

New Zealand

Southern Ocean